EUTHANASIA AND PHYSICIAN-ASSISTED SUICIDE ■
Killing or Caring?

by

Michael Manning, M.D.

Paulist Press
New York/Mahwah, N.J.

Cover design by Cynthia Dunne

Interior design by Joseph E. Petta

Library of Congress Cataloging-in-Publication Data

Manning, Michael, M.D.
    Euthanasia and physician-assisted suicide : killing or caring? / by Michael Manning.
        p.   cm.
    Includes bibliographical references (p.).
    ISBN 0-8091-3804-2 (alk. paper)
    1. Euthanasia—Religious aspects—Catholic Church. 2. Assisted suicide—Religious aspects—Catholic Church. 3. Euthanasia—Religious aspects. 4. Assisted suicide—Religious aspects. I. Title.
R726.M315   1998
179.7—dc21   98-17655
                                                                                      CIP

Published by Paulist Press
997 Macarthur Boulevard
Mahwah, New Jersey 07430

Printed and bound in the
United States of America

Contents ■

Now is the time for the medical profession to rally in defense of its fundamental moral principles, to repudiate any and all acts of direct and intentional killing by physicians and their agents.

Willard Gaylin, M.D., Leon R. Kass, M.D.,
Edmund D. Pellegrino, M.D., Mark Siegler, M.D.
Doctors Must Not Kill

Those who work in the medical profession...ought to neglect no means of making all their skill available to the sick and the dying; but they should also remember how much more necessary it is to provide them with the comfort of boundless kindness and heartfelt charity.

Congregation for the Doctrine of the Faith
Declaration on Euthanasia

The health care profession is meant to be an impassioned and unflinching affirmation of life.

John Paul II
Evangelium vitae

To the Seminary Community at
St. Mary's Seminary & University

Preface ■

FIVE YEARS AGO, while browsing through current periodicals in the seminary library, I discovered an article that discussed the medical research performed by Nazi physicians on concentration camp inmates. It sickened me. The extent of physician involvement in the Nazi killing machine shocked me. I read what additional scholarly materials I could find and attempted to trace the medical involvement back to its roots; it seemed to have begun with euthanasia of those born with congenital anomalies. Other than deflating any moral self-righteousness I felt as a physician, my new insights seemed to have little practical consequence—that is, until "right-to-die" initiatives began appearing on state ballots and Jack Kevorkian began making house calls in Michigan.

I returned to the literature and read the newly published materials. The more I read, the more alarmed I became. I learned euthanasia has been an issue since antiquity, not spawned as a by-product of modern life-sustaining technology, as I had believed. Paradoxically, this might be a reason for optimism that a perennial problem might continue to be successfully kept at bay.

I became alarmed because I learned more about the technological detachment and efficiency of the German physicians who collaborated with the Nazis during World War II. First they euthanized the congenitally handicapped, next the insane and the elderly, then, on a massive scale, the "undesirables" in an extermination that was thoroughly medicalized. I was repulsed by detailed accounts of grotesque medical experiments performed on human beings by German physicians. I felt intense shame for the profession perverted so thoroughly by Nazi propaganda; much less secure about the integrity and code of ethics of the medical profession; less confident that as a group, physicians will always "do good and avoid evil."

I read the accounts of euthanasia in the Netherlands incredulously—physicians and families euthanizing patients, sometimes with less remorse than when we put our aged family dog "to sleep." I found the routine admissions by Dutch doctors that they euthanize patients without their specific consent equally appalling. In the midst of legislative and judicial battles in the United States over the legalization of euthanasia and physician-assisted suicide, some surveys of physicians report that "only" one-third of physicians polled would be willing to participate in some form of euthanasia or physician-assisted suicide. In my opinion, there is cause for much concern.

I believe the evidence leads to the conclusion that we must not legalize euthanasia or physician-assisted suicide. Instead, our society should mobilize a life-giving health care system that includes compassionate care for the dying, adequate analgesia and human comforts near the end of life, and widespread education about the right to refuse burdensome medical care.

Here I will examine only the broad moral and ethical issues of euthanasia and physician-assisted suicide as they pertain to medicine and theology. No attempt is made to examine jurisprudence in detail or focus on the specific legislative initiatives either legalizing or banning these practices. The thorny philosophical and religious issue of "personhood " is not discussed, nor are the various proposals to redefine death, though all these issues also have important ramifications for care near the end of life. The basic arguments for and against euthanasia and physician-assisted suicide have remained surprisingly unchanged for centuries; I will focus attention on these.

I thank those with whom I lived at St. Mary's Seminary in Baltimore for their patience in listening to each day's newest "discovery" and for their forbearance of my darker moods while I was researching the Nazi Holocaust. For the friendships I made during five years of priestly formation, I am forever grateful.

I thank Fr. Phil Keane, S.S., and Fr. Tom Ulshafer, S.S., for their helpful suggestions on this manuscript and their encouragement to pursue studies in medical ethics.

Chapter 1 ■
Introduction

THE DEBATE OVER EUTHANASIA is becoming more strident at least in part because there is confusion about the terminology describing the care at the end of life. The term *euthanasia,* as we will see, originally meant only "good death," but in modern society it has come to mean a death free of any anxiety and pain, often brought about through the use of medication. Most recently, it has come to mean "mercy killing"—deliberately putting an end to someone's life in order to spare the individual's suffering.

In the *Declaration on Euthanasia,* the Congregation for the Doctrine of the Faith states:

> By euthanasia is understood an action or an omission which of itself or by intention causes death, in order that all suffering may in this way be eliminated. Euthanasia's terms of reference, therefore, are to be found in the intention of the will and in the methods used.[1]

Originally, *passive euthanasia* meant the avoidance of extreme or heroic measures to prolong life in the case of incurable and painful terminal illness. Its advocates maintained that treatment should be withheld not to hasten death, but to avoid the pain and

rapid ·

suffering of prolonged dying. In more contemporary usage, the term is sometimes used to mean the *withdrawal* of medical treatment. *Active euthanasia,* on the other hand, is a deliberate intervention, by someone other than the person whose life is at stake, solely intended to end his or her life. It is *voluntary* when such a request is made by a competent, terminally ill patient who makes a fully voluntary and persistent request for aid in dying. *Involuntary* active euthanasia is an intervention intended to kill a person who is incapable of making a request to die: an infant, young child, or mentally incompetent patient; or someone who, because of impaired consciousness, is unable to give voice to his or her opinions.

Recent papal documents and some Catholic ethicists prefer to avoid the term *passive euthanasia.* Forgoing or withdrawing medical treatment that offers no hope of benefit to the total well-being of the patient, or that imposes burdens disproportionate to the potential benefits, *allows the patient to die.* This is perfectly acceptable in Catholic teaching because its primary intention is not to cause death, but to either avoid a prolonged course of dying or to avoid a serious threat to the physical, psychological, spiritual, or economic well-being of the individual. Death may be predictable, even inevitable as a result of the action, but it is not directly intended.

While the Church would call this allowing the patient to die, some would call it passive euthanasia. The same action—removing a respirator, for example—could be morally permitted or not, depending on the moral intention of those removing the respirator.[2] If the intent was to allow the patient to die, it is permitted; if the intent was to kill the patient, it is not. This important distinction will be discussed in more detail in chapter 5. For now, it is simply enough to note that one must clearly understand what each author means by the term *passive euthanasia.*

In physician-assisted suicide, the physician may provide the patient with the means to end his or her life, but the patient performs the lethal act himself or herself. Generally speaking, the physician is not present and may not be aware of the exact time and place of the patient's death. Typically, the physician would provide a prescription for a generous supply of short-acting phenobarbiturate, probably with some instructions on how to consume the medication in order to ensure a fatal outcome.[3] Physician-assisted suicide may not be morally different from euthanasia, and need not be distinguished from euthanasia for purposes of understanding the moral vision and values at stake in the euthanasia debate.[4] Many physicians, however, believe that there is a difference, and surveys have generally shown that a greater percentage of physicians are willing to cooperate in their patients' suicides than are willing to perform active euthanasia. Whether a physician provides a lethal prescription or personally administers the lethal drug, the moral intent is the same—the premature death of the patient. While we may differ on how to apportion moral responsibility for the death of the patient in each case, the basic issue is still premature patient death—whether physician-assisted or self-inflicted.

Table 1. Definitions Related to Euthanasia[5]

Term	Definition
Voluntary active euthanasia	Intentionally administering medications to cause the patient's death at the patient's request and with full, informed consent
Involuntary active euthanasia	Intentionally administering medications to cause the patient's death without the patient's request and full, informed consent

Passive euthanasia	Witholding or withdrawing life-sustaining medical treatments from a patient *with the intent of causing death*
Physician-assisted suicide	A physician providing medications or other means to a patient with the understanding that the patient intends to use them to commit suicide

The euthanasia and physician-assisted suicide debate can be summed up as follows: Is it morally acceptable, and so ought it be legally permissible, for a physician to take the life of a competent, terminally ill patient who requests it, or for a physician to assist the competent, terminally ill patient in taking his or her own life?

Since many of the arguments for or against euthanasia and physician-assisted suicide are closely related, they are difficult to discuss one at a time. Before examining the major themes in the euthanasia debate, it is helpful to trace the history of euthanasia. We will do this in two parallel time lines: first, its development in secular history; and second, its development within the Roman Catholic tradition and magisterial documents, especially in the recent teachings of Pope John Paul II. With this background, the arguments for and against euthanasia will be grouped around several broad themes. How does the concept of individual autonomy impact the euthanasia debate? Might compassionate care for the dying include mercifully killing them? This leads to a discussion of a crucial distinction in Roman Catholic medical ethics: the distinction between killing and allowing to die.

We will examine the concept of the "common good" to see what help it may give in framing the limits of the debate. Next we look at the slippery slope argument, not only in its theoretical form, but also at the possible psychological and sociological impact of allowing exceptions to our rules against euthanasia. A review of some real-life "slippery slopes" will be done to help assess the strengths and weaknesses of this argument: How was euthanasia practiced in Nazi Germany, and is this related to its current practice in the Netherlands? Are there professional standards intrinsic to the practice of medicine that either permit or prohibit euthanasia and physician-assisted suicide? I will conclude with my own viewpoint on the debate, including an assessment of the most cogent arguments against euthanasia in a pluralistic society.

Chapter 2 ■
History of Euthanasia

Euthanasia in Greece and Rome

IN CLASSICAL GREEK ANTIQUITY and into the pre-Christian era of the Roman Empire, the term *euthanasia* did not have the narrow, technical meaning we apply to it today. The ancients focused not on the act of hastening death itself, but rather on the manner of one's dying. The important thing was for the dying person to meet death with peace of mind and minimal pain. It was essential that death be met in a psychologically balanced state of mind, under composed circumstances, in a condition of self-control. To ensure such a death, it was permissible to arrange the circumstances surrounding one's death, including measures that would shorten one's life.[6]

Many ancient Greeks and Romans preferred "voluntary death over endless agony. This form of euthanasia was an everyday reality...and many physicians actually gave their patients the poison for which they were asked."[7] A "good death" was not anchored in a medical context alone, nor did euthanasia carry the negative connotation of *suicide*. The ancients stressed the voluntary nature of the dying, provided that it was done for the right reasons; for example, to end the suffering of a terminal illness.[8] Indeed, in classical Athens, the city magistrates kept a supply of poison for anyone who wished to die: "If your life is hateful to you, die; if you are overwhelmed by fate, drink the hemlock."[9]

The Stoics, a Greek philosophical movement that professed a divinely authored cosmic plan to which the individual needed to resign oneself, endorsed euthanasia when the person's life was no longer in accord with his or her individual felt needs and self-knowledge.[10] Two conditions were necessary for acceptable euthanasia: (1) the person's motivation had to fit an acceptable category, for example, victimization by chronic or incurable disease; and (2) the person had to weigh his or her responsibilities to others. Euthanasia was not to be taken as a means to avoid life's responsibilities.[11] The Stoic founder, Zeno, apparently committed suicide in his old age due to the "agonizing pain of a foot injury."[12]

Not all ancient philosophers accepted the practice of active voluntary euthanasia, however. The Pythagoreans opposed it since they believed the gods valued each human soul—euthanasia disrespected human life. Earthly existence, furthermore, was seen as a punishment for past sins, therefore it must not be prematurely ended. To artificially terminate one's life was a violation of the god's commands. It is unclear, however, whether the Pythagoreans believed that human life had intrinsic worth, or if its value was derived solely from the commands of the gods.

Plato, too, opposed suicide, though he was generally sympathetic to euthanasia in cases of agonizing or debilitating illness. He rejected the idea that the right to take life belonged to the gods alone, and insisted that life could be ended by the individual in cases of imminent death, or when the person's ability to perform his duties to the state was essentially lost. In Plato's view, the chronically ill and disabled were useless both to themselves and to the state.[13] Aristotle, on the other hand, opposed euthanasia not only because it prematurely deprived the state of one of its productive members, but because it was cowardly. Facing death courageously was an important test of moral virtue.[14]

The question of the physician's role in helping to fulfill a patient's request for aid in dying arose early in the classical period. Socrates saw nothing wrong when a physician failed to postpone the dying process. He praised Asclepius, god of healing and medicine, for his humane and practical policies:

> He [Asclepius] did not want to lengthen out the good-for-nothing lives.... Those who are diseased,...[physicians] will leave to die, and the corrupt and incurable souls they will put an end to themselves.[15]

A minority of physicians challenged this widespread acceptance of euthanasia. These were the adherents of the Hippocratic school who pledged "never to give a deadly drug to anybody if asked for it, nor...make a suggestion to this effect."[16]

It appears, however, that given the socially accepted notion of a "good death," it was relatively common for a physician to end the life of one of his patients, as long as he had the patient's consent. Many people preferred early voluntary death to the fear of a long, painful one; at least some physicians either gave their patients the poison for which they asked, or administered it themselves at the patient's request.[17]

It would be misleading to conclude that the ethics of the Hippocratic oath represented the ancient-day practice of the typical medical practitioner. Paul Carrick, author of a study on medical ethics in antiquity, claims that "most physicians were not even aware of the oath's existence." Those who were, felt free to adapt or modify whatever of its provisions they could. Carrick draws the following picture of ancient medical practice:

> The Hippocratic healer of the fifth and fourth centuries was never morally bound by positive duties to assist in abortion or voluntary euthanasia on request. He could, of course, assist in these practices without much risk of moral disapprobation from either

inside or outside the ranks of his craft, if he so chose. Therefore, he possessed what may be described as a *discretionary* professional right to assist in abortion or voluntary euthanasia: he was not obliged *qua* physician either to take part or to refrain from such services. It was entirely up to his own judgment and moral sense of things.[18]

Post-Classical Period

The ascendancy of Christianity, with its view that human life is a trust from God, reinforced the views of the Hippocratic school. By the twelfth through fifteenth centuries, it culminated in the near unanimity of medical opinion in opposing euthanasia. One of the earliest theoretical discussions of euthanasia in English literature was presented by Sir Thomas More in his *Utopia*, first published in 1516. In More's vision of the ideal society:

> [I]f a disease is not only incurable but also distressing and agonizing without cessation, then the priests and the public officials...exhort the man...to free himself from this bitter life...or else voluntarily permit others to free him....[19]

Although the English term had not yet been coined, More clearly refers to what we would now call active euthanasia. He did not advocate euthanasia, however, and never imagined abandoning the terminally ill to their suffering. The Utopians, on the other hand,

> do not hesitate to prescribe euthanasia;...still, the Utopians do not do away with anyone without his permission, nor lessen any of their duties to him.[20]

9

Somewhat later, Sir Francis Bacon (1561–1626) wrote that it is the physician's responsibility to reduce or alleviate the patient's pain not only when it might lead to recovery, but also when it "may serve a fair and easy passage."[21] Bacon's comments attracted little attention.

The Eighteenth-Century Enlightenment and Beyond

No serious discussion of euthanasia was even possible in Christian Europe until the eighteenth-century Enlightenment. Suddenly, writers assaulted the church's authoritative teaching on all matters, including euthanasia and suicide. David Hume (1711–76) wrote a bold but little noticed statement in his *On Suicide:*

[That] suicide may often be consistent with interest and with our duty to ourselves, no one can question, who allows that age, sickness, or misfortune, may render life a burden, and make it worse even than annihilation.[22]

While writers challenged the authority of the church with regard to ethical matters, there was no real widespread interest in the issues of euthanasia or physician-assisted suicide during that time.

An important milestone in the euthanasia debate was the isolation of morphine in the nineteenth century and its widespread use as an analgesic. Soon after John Warren performed the first operation under anesthesia, he speculated that ether might be used "in mitigating the agonies of death" and wrote a case report of its successful use in alleviating "with perfect relief" the "pain of mortification" of a 90-year-old woman.

The analgesic use of injectable morphine spread during the U.S. Civil War. By 1866, the *British Medical Journal* detailed the use of ether, chloroform, and morphine to manage the pain of death, but not necessarily to end the patient's life.

When the practice of analgesia had become reasonably well established, Samuel Williams, a nonphysician, began to advocate the use of these drugs not only to alleviate terminal pain, but to intentionally end a patient's life. Williams's viewpoint received widespread attention. He articulated his view during the Enlightenment's "Gilded Age," a period that valued laissez-faire economics, rationalism, and the scientific method in lieu of unquestioning acceptance of traditional authority.[23] Charles Darwin's groundbreaking *The Origin of the Species,* published in 1859, continued the trend toward questioning traditional authority. Social scientists rushed to incorporate his "survival of the fittest" theory into economics and sociology. This biological and social philosophy may have promoted the idea that society should assist its weakest members to end their lives, not for merciful motives, but for economic and eugenic ones.

During the late 1800s, Williams's euthanasia proposal received serious attention in medical journals and at scientific meetings. Still, most physicians held the view that pain medication could be administered to alleviate pain, but not to hasten death. The *Journal of the American Medical Association* attacked Williams's euthanasia proposal as an attempt to make "the physician don the robes of an executioner."[24]

The debate widened to include not only physicians, but also lawyers and social scientists. Attorney Alfred Bach endorsed euthanasia in 1895, arguing that patients should have a right to end their lives. Others decried the arrogance of increasingly powerful doctors, who could prolong lives at "any cost of discomfort or pain to the sufferer."[25]

By the turn of the century, medical science had made great strides. As physicians who used the modern scientific method and modern principles of pharmacology consolidated their control over university and medical school training, the euthanasia debate entered the lay press and political forums. In 1905–1906, a bill to legalize euthanasia was defeated in the Ohio legislature by a vote of 79 to 23. In 1906, a similar initiative that would legalize euthanasia not only for terminal adults, but also for "hideously deformed or idiotic children" was introduced and defeated as well. After 1906, the public interest in euthanasia receded. This was due in part to medicine's newly won autonomy over its universities and professional standards of practice and society's more beneficent view toward the economically disadvantaged.[26]

In the 1930s, debate over euthanasia revived.[27] In 1935, the confession of an anonymous British physician that he had performed euthanasia on five patients fueled the euthanasia debate on both sides of the Atlantic.[28] In 1938, a bill sponsored by the Euthanasia Society of America was defeated in the New York State Legislature. The Society believed that "with adequate safeguards, it should be made legal to allow incurable sufferers to choose immediate death rather than await it in agony."[29] Even though the bill was defeated, it rekindled interest in the subject. Abraham Wolbarst authored an article "The Doctor Looks at Euthanasia," in which he stated: "The vast majority of thinking people favor euthanasia as a humanitarian principle.… The human mind revolts at the thought of unnecessary suffering.… It is not how long we humans live, but *how* we live that is important."[30]

The euthanasia debate was not limited to this side of the Atlantic. A bill to legalize euthanasia was debated in the British House of Lords in 1936, but was rejected 35 to 14, partly because two lords who were also physicians spoke in vigorous opposition to the bill. The defeat of this bill, along with the outbreak of World War II, the subsequent discovery of the Nazi death camps, and the recognition of the complicity of the German physicians in the extermination camps quelled but did not eliminate discussion of the euthanasia question.

In the immediate wake of World War II, the euthanasia debate remained reasonably quiet. In 1947, for example, a Gallup poll revealed that only 37 percent of those Americans questioned approved of a physician being authorized to end a patient's life by some painless means if the family requested it. But in the 1960s, Louis Kutner's proposal for a patient-instigated directive, the so-called living will, revived the "death with dignity" movement.[31]

Since the 1970s in the Netherlands, and the late 1980s in the United States, the euthanasia debate has once again begun to gather momentum. During these years, patients and their surrogates have fought for and won the right to refuse unwanted medical interventions and life-prolonging measures.

In 1991, the federal Patient Self-Determination Act (PSDA) went into effect. This act mandates that every health care facility receiving Medicare or Medicaid funding—hospitals, nursing homes, health maintenance organizations (HMOs), and home-health care programs—must inform their patients or their clients of their right to decline unwanted medical treatments, including those which potentially prolong life.[32] In addition to informing individuals of their right to accept or refuse medical or surgical treatment and to prepare advance directives for their health care, facilities must apprise patients and residents of any written policies regarding implementation of these rights.

The legislation was introduced by Senators John C. Danforth and Daniel Patrick Moynihan in order to empower people to take part in the decisions that affect the duration and condition of their lives. Senator Danforth believed that providing more information to patients about their rights to refuse treatment and other options would prevent health care institutions from "neglecting the caring component of medicine and trampling on the rights of patients."[33] Written information describing the legal rights of patients to manage their own health care decisions must be provided by hospitals at the time of inpatient admission, by nursing homes when admitted as a resident, by home health agencies and HMOs when the patient enrolls, and by hospices when care is first given. The law does *not* require individuals to complete advance directives. The intent was to widely disseminate information and to educate about advance care directives.[34]

While these efforts, supported by most health care professionals, went forward, a parallel movement for the legalization of active euthanasia resumed as well. The Hemlock Society in America and the EXIT groups in Great Britain began this movement, and members of both societies published widely circulated "suicide recipe books."[35]

During this time euthanasia and physician-assisted suicide also became a moral and medical issue of increasing importance to doctors. In 1988, the *Journal of the American Medical Association* published "It's All Over, Debbie."[36] The letter details an anonymous, over-tired, "on call" gynecology resident's unilateral decision to inject a terminally ill, but alert, patient with a fatal overdose of morphine. The patient had experienced difficulty sleeping due to labored respirations for each of several successive evenings, and she told the busy resident, "Let's get this over with." In response, he administered a fatal dose of morphine. The reaction to the article was strong and swift against not only the anonymous physician, who was labeled a murderer by some of his colleagues, but also against the medical journal for publishing the article. In a bluntly worded article criticizing the resident's action, three physicians expressed the opinion that the resident had broken the law, breached medical protocol, and violated the most deeply held and hallowed canon of medical ethics: Doctors must not kill.[37]

Within one year, "The Physician's Responsibility Toward Hopelessly Ill Patients" was published.[38] Authored by twelve physicians from leading medical centers across the United States, ten of its authors believed "that it is not immoral for a physician to assist in the rational suicide of a terminally ill patient," although the group stopped short of advocating active euthanasia.[39] Their motivation for such discretion may have been due to fear of malpractice litigation: "The social climate in this country is very litigious, and the likelihood of prosecution if a case of euthanasia were discovered is fairly high—much higher than the likelihood of prosecution after a suicide in which the physician has assisted."[40] Whether or not the authors really wished to endorse physician-assisted suicide, they opened the debate on euthanasia and physician-assisted suicide in reputable professional circles.

Even though we may presume that advances in medical technology have sharpened the arguments, both pro and con, in the euthanasia debate, it is surprising to learn that the arguments for and against euthanasia have changed little over this century. The physician-ethicist Ezekiel Emanuel reviews some of the major themes, noting that the arguments have changed little in the past years: "...articles written on the topic in 1894 could be dated 1994."[41] These debates center around autonomy, drawing a distinction between allowing to die and actively causing death, finding a moral equivalence between withdrawing life support and failing to initiate it, the principle of double effect, and either alleging or denying that legalizing euthanasia would set us on a slippery slope.

As Emanuel points out, the debate over euthanasia was framed from the earliest days of medicine, well before any significant technology was available to forestall death (e.g., mechanical ventilation, intravenous pressors, extracorporeals pumps, renal dialysis, etc.). In his view, social pressures, not high-tech medicine, are responsible for the interest in euthanasia. Social

Darwinism, ("survival of the fittest"), economic recession, laissez-faire politics and the championing of individual rights are some examples of such social pressures. Emmanuel contends that significant interest in euthanasia arises whenever the authority of physicians is severely challenged. "The interest in euthanasia may be a public condemnation of physician control over patients' deaths....Thus the current interest in euthanasia may be the culmination of the twenty-year effort to curtail physician authority over end-of-life decisions."[42]

Interestingly, the medical profession and science itself may now be the focus of the same kind of anti-authoritarian criticism aimed at the church in the 1700s. Although science led the charge against established forms of authority then, modern philosophers now focus their criticism on the scientific method and science itself.

History of Euthanasia in Church Teaching/Documents

Since its earliest days, the church has condemned the taking of innocent human life. However, suicide to escape intolerable suffering has been a perennial problem. *The Shepherd of Hermas* (probably written between 140–55 C.E.) urged that adequate care be provided for the poor lest they resort to suicide. During the Roman persecutions, pagans taunted Christians for cowardice, since if they really believed in life after death they should kill themselves to get there more quickly. Justin Martyr deflected such taunts, maintaining that Christians more properly obey God by living in the world and preaching the Gospel.[43]

St. Augustine spoke out directly against suicide. The commandment "Thou shalt not kill" admitted no exceptions. The "suicides" of some biblical figures and of some martyrs were "either authorized by God or due to excusable but mistaken enthusiasm."[44]

Augustine held that life and its suffering were divinely ordained by God and must be borne accordingly. A human was created in the image of God, and his or her life thus belonged to God. The time and manner of death was God's will alone.[45]

Augustine's prohibitions against suicide became accepted by the monks of the Middle Ages and set a standard for the moralists of the period. These prohibitions became codified in the moral manuals of the high middle ages.

Later, Thomas Aquinas grounded the prohibition philosophically. His general approach has been called the theory of natural law, which claims that human reason alone can arrive at the truth revealed to us by God in sufficient detail to "do good and avoid evil" in particular moral dilemmas. He began with Augustine's assertion of God's fundamental dominion over all lives. Thomas prefaced this argument with two others. First, suicide inherently contradicts the intrinsic motivation of all life to preserve itself; second, it is politically unjust because it deprives the community of the life of one of its members.

These arguments may sound familiar; they are essentially Aristotle's. Suicide violates the love of God, self, and community. Aquinas viewed the universe as created by God and ordered by intrinsically consistent laws, so it is important to note that the biblical commandment "Thou shalt not kill" is placed alongside two further arguments, which operate from the nature and ends of the human person and the human community. While Aristotle accepted the legitimacy of ending "useless" life, Aquinas maintained the sanctity of all life, regardless of its quality. Euthanasia is wrong not only because God commands it, but because it violates the meaning of the human person and the nature of a human community.

Given these proscriptions against taking human life, Christians reinterpreted the Greek and Roman sense of a "good death." Now it came to mean tranquillity and resignation in accepting death.

Suffering was not pointless. God could use suffering as a means of producing spiritual maturity; patient suffering could be trans-formative and salvific. While the sufferer was obliged to endure patiently, there was a concomitant obligation on the part of one's fellow Christians to console and encourage the sufferer. Even though Christian charity brought the obligation to relieve suffer-ing, this was *not* to be done by killing the terminally suffering. The biblical commandment not to kill seemed even to prohibit killing done for motives of mercy.[46]

In the Renaissance and during the Reformation, arguments against the church's teaching on euthanasia surfaced alongside objections to church authority in general. Francis Bacon intro-duced the term *euthanasia* in a plea for physicians to do more to ease the suffering of the dying, but without openly defending actual mercy killing.

The moral arguments against euthanasia are found in the moral manuals of the period. The Jesuit Juan Cardinal deLugo, who helped develop the distinction between ordinary and extra-ordinary medical care, adduced four arguments against it: (1) God, not humans, has dominion over human life; (2) suicide is an injustice to the community; (3) it is contrary to the natural love we owe ourselves; and (4) it is cowardly. DeLugo found the first argument the most persuasive, and he largely followed Thomas's lead in arguing against euthanasia.[47]

Cardinal deLugo nuanced Aquinas' interpretation of our oblig-ations. He noted our "perfect" obligation not to take innocent human life, but a merely "positive" obligation of Christians to pre-serve life. This positive obligation was often ambiguous and open-ended. Even though it was clear that the Christian is not obligated to do everything possible to preserve life, it was not clear exactly what means were obligatory. Further, our dominion over our own lives, though broad, is not unlimited. Since we do not possess total dominion over our own lives, we are forbidden to take it by suicide. Yet the means we are obliged to use in order to preserve it must be balanced by our other obligations, by the fact that our earthly lives are finite, and by God's ultimate dominion over all creation.[48]

Following Aquina's and deLugo's lead, theologians have struggled to clarify the distinction between obligatory or ordinary medical care and nonobligatory or optional treatments. Archbishop Daniel A. Cronin's doctoral dissertation reviews the concept of *extraordinary* and *ordinary* in magisterial teaching. Though many contemporary writers prefer the terms *proportionate* and *disproportionate,* Cronin's analysis is a helpful tool for making treatment decisions.

Theologian Kevin Wildes discusses five criteria of extraordinary means used by Cronin and other Catholic moralists:

1. Impossibility: Reasonable judgments of prudent and conscientious individuals determine that the proposed treatment constitutes a moral impossibility.
2. Excessive effort: The classic example is the need to take a long journey to live in a more healthful climate (in the Middle Ages, pilgrimages themselves were hazardous to one's health). One is not bound to submit to an extremely dangerous operation or a burdensome convalescence.
3. Pain: Modern techniques of analgesia and anesthesia should make this a lesser consideration than in earlier days. Nevertheless, properly treated but intractable pain, or the ongoing pain and discomfort of chemotherapy or dialysis, for example, would still be pertinent.
4. Expense: The patient's means and socioeconomic status must be taken into account here. This distinction must not, however, be used to justify purely economic discrimination in health care delivery, nor to sanction multiple standards of care based on socioeconomic status.

5. <u>Fear and repugnance</u> *(vehemens horror):* Fear, even if unwarranted and irrational, may make a means extraordinary. Fear of renal dialysis or living with the results of an amputation could render either treatment extraordinary.

Ordinary means are those we are morally required to take. Ordinary does not mean "common" or "usual" in this context. For means to be obligatory they must: (1) offer some reasonable hope of benefit; (2) be part of the normal standard of care; (3) be consistent with a person's social position and status (a religious novice could not be required to leave his or her religious community to seek more healthy medical treatment); and (4) not be excessively difficult. This includes expense, pain, danger, fear, etc. All these factors serve to balance the obligation to preserve one's life against the proportionate difficulty of fulfilling this obligation.[49]

From the earliest period then, we see the church defending innocent human life and insisting that control over even our own lives is limited by God's universal dominion. Because of the passion, death, and resurrection of Jesus, human suffering could be salvific. Despite the sanctity of human life, extraordinary means to preserve it are not mandatory.

Religious History—Theological and Magisterial Documents

No comprehensive statements about euthanasia were made by ecumenical councils or popes prior to Pius XII. This may reflect the relatively tranquil state of Catholic moral theology from the time of Trent to Vatican II. When, however, the German National Socialists adopted "eugenic euthanasia," Pius XII wrote:

Conscious of the obligations of our high office, we deem it necessary to reiterate this grave statement today, when to our profound grief we see the bodily-deformed, the insane, and those suffering from hereditary disease at times deprived of their lives, as though they were a useless burden to society. And this procedure is hailed by some as a new discovery of human progress, as something that is altogether justified by the common good. Yet what sane man does not recognize that this not only violates the natural and divine law written in the heart of every man, but flies in the face of every sensibility of civilized humanity? The blood of these victims, all the dearer to our Redeemer because deserving of greater pity, "cries to God from the earth" (Gn 4:10).[50]

In several other addresses the pope also condemned voluntary euthanasia as a violation of God's sole dominion over innocent life, and as a refusal to accept unitive suffering with Christ.[51] In his address to anesthesiologists, he reasserted that there was no moral obligation to apply every life-saving measure regardless of burden or benefit, and he permitted the use of end-stage narcotic pain relief, even if it hastened the advance of death (a simple statement of the classic double effect).

Vatican II condemned "crimes against life" such as genocide, abortion, euthanasia, and willful suicide, but did not define euthanasia or discuss it any detail, perhaps because it was not then a volatile issue.[52] Some speculate that Nazi eugenics and the human medical experiments on prisoners of war quelled discussion of euthanasia in the wake of World War II.[53] But as wartime memories faded and the "death with dignity" movements began to pick up momentum both in the United States and in Europe, John Paul II found it necessary to issue teachings on the subject. The Congregation for the Doctrine of the Faith's *Declaration on Euthanasia* is the first and fullest direct statement on the subject ever made by the magisterium.

It is necessary to state firmly once more that nothing and no one can in any way permit the killing of an innocent human being, whether a fetus or an embryo, an infant or an adult, an old person, or one suffering from an incurable disease, or a person who is dying. Furthermore, no one is permitted to ask for this act of killing, either for himself or herself or for another person entrusted to his or her care, nor can he or she consent to it, either explicitly or implicitly. Nor can any authority legitimately recommend or permit such an action. For it is a question of the violation of the divine law, an offense against the dignity of the human person, a crime against life, and an attack on humanity.[54]

Catholic teaching views human life as a gift of God's love, a gift we are called upon to preserve and make fruitful as stewards. Intentionally causing one's own death is equally as wrong as killing another. The classic prohibitions against suicide are maintained for euthanasia: It fails to fulfill one's responsibility to God, violates one's own natural desire to exist, betrays self-love, and injures one's community.[55]

Alarmed by what he called a "culture of death," Pope John Paul II saw the need for a broad-based, philosophically consistent defense of the sanctity of human life. In 1995, the pope promulgated *Evangelium vitae,* in which he decried all assaults on the dignity of human life, singling out the direct taking of innocent human life, abortion, and euthanasia for special emphasis.

In harmony with the magisterium of my predecessors and in communion with the bishops of the Catholic Church, I confirm that euthanasia is a grave violation of the law of God, since it is the deliberate and morally unacceptable killing of a human person. This doctrine is based upon the natural law and upon the written word of God, is transmitted by the church's tradition, and taught by the ordinary and universal magisterium.[56]

22

This encyclical contains the definitive teachings of John Paul II on euthanasia, and it will be explored here at some length. In it the pope points out that when life is valued only when it brings pleasure and well being, suffering can be seen as something from which to escape at all costs. Humans usurp God's sovereignty when, through the use of euthanasia, they propose to bring about death before its time.

John Paul II defines euthanasia as an action or omission that of itself and by intention causes death, with the purpose of eliminating all suffering. He continues to draw a distinction between euthanasia and the permissible decision to forgo "aggressive medical treatments," either because they become disproportionate to any expected results, or because they impose an excessive burden on the patient and his or her family. The pope confirms that euthanasia is a grave violation of the law of God, since it is the deliberate and morally unacceptable killing of a human person. He emphasizes that this prohibition is based on the natural law, upon scripture, church tradition, and teaching of the ordinary and universal magisterium.

The pope asserts that the term *mercy killing* is a misnomer; instead, it is mercy perverted. True compassion leads to sharing another's pain, not to killing him or her to end it. He cites particularly the practice of ending the life of another who has not even requested it (involuntary euthanasia), a practice unfortunately not uncommon in the Netherlands. The healthy and powerful have a social obligation to protect the sick and suffering; their use of euthanasia perverts the social order. The pope warns that euthanasia could be used as a tool of oppression.

John Paul II reaffirms church teaching that our dominion over human life is limited by God's divine sovereignty. In commenting on the relationship between the political and the moral order, he asserts that no human law can claim to legitimize euthanasia, and that citizens are under no obligation to obey such laws.

Indeed they have a moral obligation to oppose them by conscientious objection. Society as a whole must respect, defend, and promote the dignity of every human person, at every moment and in every condition of that person's life.

When suffering cannot be alleviated, it should not be viewed as pointless or debasing. The sanctity of human life is not diminished by human suffering. On the contrary, love gives meaning to suffering and death. Human life is sacred and remains inviolable—a gift of God.

> Suffering is present in the world in order to release love, in order to give birth to works of love towards neighbor, in order to transform the whole of human civilization into a "civilization of love."

But with the passion of Christ, "all human suffering has found itself in a new situation."[57] The pope calls suffering "a call. It is a vocation." While the reasons for human suffering, (the theodicy question) are not explained, Christ gives an example, invoked with his invitation, "Follow me!"[58] When human sufferings are united to the redemptive suffering of Christ, they provide a special support for "the powers of good" and open the door to "the victory of these salvific powers."[59]

In light of this understanding of suffering, John Paul II calls on physicians to conscientiously oppose euthanasia. He claims that causing death can never be considered a form of medical treatment, even when the intention is solely to comply with the patient's request. It runs completely counter to the health care profession, which is meant to be an impassioned and unflinching affirmation of life.

The pope reiterates the Catholic teaching that "aggressive medical treatment" need not be utilized. He defines such treatment as medical procedures that no longer correspond to the real situation of the patient, either because they are disproportionate to expected results, or because they impose an excessive burden on the patient and his or her family. To forgo extraordinary or disproportionate means is not the equivalent of suicide or euthanasia, but rather expresses the acceptance of the mortality of the human condition. John Paul II explicitly reaffirms the teaching of Pius XII that permits the use of narcotics to relieve pain, even when the result is decreased consciousness or shortening of life. He insists, however, that no other means of controlling the pain must be available, that the performance of other religious and moral duties is not prevented (such as making a final confession), and that the individual must not be deprived of consciousness without a serious reason.

The method of argumentation used in *Evangelium vitae* is much the same as other encyclicals of John Paul II: The pope assumes the traditional natural law teachings of Catholic theology on particular points, uses a scripturally based theme (Cain and Abel in this encyclical), and then comments on contemporary cultural trends. On the major points of murder, abortion, and euthanasia he explicitly confirms the existing teaching. The position on the death penalty is more strongly negative than in other papal encyclicals, but consistent with this pontiff's recent emphases.

We can see that John Paul II accepts a teleological view of the medical profession (it is directed toward a specific goal, i.e., its aim is healing), rejects the patient autonomy model (at least on the issue of euthanasia), and in affirming the inviolable sanctity of human life at all stages, implicitly accepts the dangers posed by allowing exceptions to the prohibitions against mercy killing.

Magisterial documents have consistently defended the sanctity of human life, speaking more explicitly to the issue of euthanasia as the practice has become more widespread. John Paul II has carefully drawn together many church teachings to mount a theologically and philosophically consistent defense of the value of human life.

Chapter 3 ■
Self-Determination

DOES AN INDIVIDUAL HAVE AN ABSOLUTE RIGHT to exercise control over his or her body? This question lies at the heart of the euthanasia debate. Some say yes and argue that this right includes the prerogative to bring one's own life to an end. Others insist that the right of an individual over even his or her own body is not absolute and does not include the right to assisted suicide or euthanasia. Let us examine each position more closely.

The self-determination, or autonomy, argument in favor of euthanasia reaches back to classical antiquity. Autonomy is the right of a person to control his or her body and life decisions. Those who hold this view argue that our liberty should include the freedom to choose our final exit. If we legally prohibit active euthanasia, we fail to respect the freedom of those who want the physician to assist them in dying. The patient who either consents to being killed or asks assistance in suicide presumably harms no other person. From this perspective, laws restricting assisted suicide or euthanasia seem paternalistic, unjustified, and arbitrary.[60]

Many Americans seem to agree that the value of self-determination extends to choosing the time and manner of one's death.[61] Sixty-five percent of those who supported the "right to die" initiative, California's Proposition 161, did so on the basis of their belief in the individual's absolute control over his or her own life and death.[62] One moral theologian has remarked that "as a society, we have a great tolerance for letting people do their own thing, even if it means seeking assistance in suicide."[63]

Most people, as Dan Brock and other commentators note, are very concerned about the manner and circumstances of their deaths. Some of their fears are fueled by modern medical technology: few want to be "trapped" on medical life-support machinery, unable to discontinue futile life-extending treatment. Support for another pro-euthanasia initiative in the state of Washington, Proposition 119, was fueled by the fear that "people have only one perception of how they die—hooked up to tubes and machines in an intensive care unit with no control."[64] Ethicist Dan Callahan has found a correlation between the increasing support for the legalization of euthanasia and the growing fear many people have of becoming trapped in unacceptable positions of dependency and disability brought about by medicine's ability to prolong dying.[65] In his view, the theoretical right to refuse life-sustaining treatment is not enough to sufficiently allay such fears.

Other fears about death are more existential. People fear losing control of the circumstances of their lives; they desire to retain as much dignity as possible by controlling the dying process.[66] Faced with the existential fear of death, the rugged individual can take control of his or her own fate and determine not only which medical treatments are appropriate and which are not, but the time and manner of death. Euthanasia advocates assert that the right of the patient to choose must be respected by all, even by the physician and even when the patient chooses death.

Modern death does not often come suddenly in the night, nor from a sudden catastrophic illness; more often it comes slowly—life is stolen away in incremental bites by chronic illness; dignity is slowly eroded by increased dependence on long-term caregivers. For many near death, the ability to maintain control over their gradual decline is extremely important. Some can adjust to their increasing infirmity and find ways to live in fulfilling and enriching ways. Others more quickly find their lives burdensome and unwanted. If self-determination is a value, then it is important that each individual be allowed to control the manner, circumstances, and time of death.

The Catholic Church has no quarrel with a properly contextualized understanding of autonomy.[67] The church, for example, defends the inviolability of a properly formed individual conscience.[68] It similarly defends the right of the individual to refuse burdensome medical treatments.[69] But the church holds that there are divine limits on the autonomy not only of individuals, but of nations and states as well.[70]

Some "pro-choice" advocates, however, place no such limits. *Choice* and *control* become important for their own sakes. Individuals have a right to make important decisions about their lives and lifestyles in pursuit of what they deem to be the good life. They should be free to act on these decisions without interference. Within the bounds of justice and so long as others are not harmed or their freedom interfered with, society ought not interfere with life-ending decisions.

One of the central aspects of human personhood and dignity is the ability to direct one's life without undue interference. Essential to this dignity is the sound mental capacity of the individual concerned: organic dementia and psychological or psychiatric factors limiting mental competence would prevent the individual from making significant end-of-life decisions. Who, if anyone, can make the decision to end life on behalf of the mentally incompetent?

American courts have tended to extend civil rights enjoyed by the competent and able-bodied to the physically and mentally handicapped by surrogates. Some argue that the "right to death" must be extended to all, even the mentally incompetent. Providing an administrative mechanism for exercising these "rights" on behalf of the handicapped may lead to involuntary euthanasia or surrogate euthanasia by judicial fiat.[71]

Most who support euthanasia as a right of self-determination allow that the right of a patient to self-determination cannot compel physicians to act contrary to their own personal moral or professional values.[72] After all, physicians' rights to self-determination must also be respected. Most who view euthanasia as a right would permit the transfer of patient care to another physician in a case where a patient wishes euthanasia but the physician disagrees with or cannot honor the decision due to personal belief.

In the Netherlands, for example, the newest government regulations concerning physician-assisted euthanasia specifically allow for conscientious objection on the part of physicians. However, according to recent statements by the chief inspector of public health for the Netherlands, he feels that if a doctor does not agree to perform euthanasia on a patient who requests it and does not promptly refer the patient to another doctor who will, the physician is guilty of malpractice and should be brought up on disciplinary charges.[73]

"Soft" patient autonomy advocates support the right of the patient to refuse unwanted medical care, a position supported by the Catholic Church. "Hard" patient autonomy advocates go further, however. They insist that the individual has a right to end his or her own life, and some maintain that patients have a right to insist that society and the physician help them fulfill their desire to die.

The fact that the physician is also an autonomous individual raises an interesting problem: The physician must also find a basis in his or her own moral system for euthanizing the patient;

he or she cannot simply act as the patient's agent and carry out the patient's wishes.

As we have seen, the Catholic Church supports the limited autonomy of the individual to make decisions and act to carry them out. This includes the right to own and dispose of private property and the right to make fundamental decisions about appropriate health care treatment, including refusal of overly burdensome treatment. For centuries, the Catholic Church has taught that this does *not* include the right to end one's own life.

Critics of those who advocate euthanasia on the grounds of self-determination contend that they have let their argument get out of hand. "Choice" has been made an inviolable transcendental: Catholic moral theologian Richard McCormick calls this the "absolutization of autonomy"; Dan Callahan calls it "self-determination run amok."[74] Even without invoking spiritual values against the autonomy argument, its critics contend that its logical conclusion is nonsensical. Carried to its extreme conclusion, the state would be unable to place any limit at all on voluntary euthanasia or assisted suicide, or on any consensual act of killing, such as dueling. Ultimate respect for a person's right to choose mandates that one's decision for suicide or euthanasia be respected, even if the person is neither facing terminal illness nor in imminent danger of death.

Critics argue that this is precisely what has already happened in several instances of Jack Kevorkian's "mercy killings." His first three assisted suicides were: (1) a functioning, lucid woman who had been newly diagnosed with Alzheimer's disease and was fearful she would slip into dementia before she could voluntarily end her life; (2) a 43-year-old woman with multiple sclerosis; and (3) a 58-year-old woman who suffered chronic pelvic pain from presumptive chronic pelvic inflammatory disease, no trace of which was found at autopsy.[75] As of this writing, Kevorkian has facilitated the deaths of nearly fifty individuals. In August of

1996, he assisted Judith Curren, a 42-year-old woman suffering from obesity and chronic fatigue syndrome to end her life.[76]

Opponents of euthanasia argue that there is a naive expectation of the degree of freedom involved in making the choice to end one's life. Those who practice clinical medicine or care for the elderly have seen many instances of elderly patients being subtly, and sometimes not so subtly, pressured by loved ones or relatives. Even if the family does not exert psychological force, the decision to request euthanasia is hardly free if the consequences of living are financial ruin or psychological or medical mistreatment. William F. May is among those who express their fears over the shortcomings of the present health care system: unequal access to health care, along with economic pressure to contain costs, may create an unhealthy pressure for euthanasia as an easy solution.[77]

Socioeconomic factors are not the only pressures that may influence inappropriate choices for euthansia or physician-assisted suicide. There is a significant psychiatric morbidity among patients requesting physician-hastened death. A significant medical literature exists outlining the complex meaning of a patient request for assisted suicide or euthanasia. Many experts recommend a thorough psychiatric screening—and treatment for organic depression when indicated—in any patient requesting euthanasia. The request for euthanasia may be a desperate cry for help, rather than for specific aid-in-dying.[78]

Herbert Hendin has made a study of the Dutch film *Death on Request*. This film was designed by the group *Compassion in Dying* to showcase the benefits of euthanasia as an expansion of patient autonomy. According to Hendin's analysis, even this idealized vision shows the coercion of the beleaguered patient—by family, physician, and film crew—to accept the "inevitable" and make the "reasonable choice" for euthanasia. We will examine the Dutch experience with euthanasia in greater detail in chapter 7.

Hendin demonstrates what he believes to be the coercion of the patient to set a date for his euthanasia and then to go through with it. Any disturbing emotion is minimized by wife and physician alike, presumably so that the patient does not become so upset that he changes his mind about euthanasia.

Death on Request depicts the euthanasia of Cees van Wendel, a patient diagnosed with amyotrophic lateral sclerosis one month prior to his euthanasia. He was confined to a wheelchair by severe muscular weakness. His speech was barely audible. His physician performed the euthanasia during a house-call while the patient's wife was present. Hendin notes:

> The wife appears repulsed by her husband's illness, never touching him during their conversation and never permitting Cees to answer any question the doctor asks directly....The doctor asks him if he wants euthanasia, but it is the wife who replies. When Cees begins to cry, the doctor moves sympathetically toward him, but his wife tells the doctor to move away and says it is better to let him cry alone....

> Throughout the film, the wife's behavior reflects her tension and fear that Cees will refuse death....Virtually the entire film is set up to avoid confronting any of the patient's feelings or how the relationship with his wife affects his agreeing to die.[79]

The second-opinion medical consultant, required by Dutch policy, asks no questions of Cees alone and accepts all of the responses given by his wife (even though Cees is able to verbalize slowly, or type on a computer keyboard). The actual euthanasia is done in a cold, clinical manner with two injections. Hendin notes that from the beginning, the husband's loneliness and isolation haunt the film. Only because he is treated from the start as an object does his death seem inevitable. The film's producer/director stated that he omitted all but one of the frequent scenes of Cees crying because "they would be too disturbing to viewers."[80] He also followed advice not to show too much footage of the patient's wife and the physician alone, for fear that it would look as though they were conspiring together. Edited and packaged, even staged as it was, Hendin asserts that the film is nothing more than "a commercial for euthanasia."[81]

Hendin's assertion that chronically ill and dependent people who say they want help in committing suicide may not always be acting out of free choice is corroborated by an entry from the diary of another spouse who "helped" his wife ingest a fatal overdose of antidepressants. The harassed husband, caretaker of his terminally ill wife, complains in his private journal: "You are sucking the life out of me like a vampire and nobody cares."[82]

As ethicist William F. May notes, a society cannot plausibly wash its hands of the practice of active euthanasia and say that the doctor's cooperation in killing is purely a private matter.[83] The doctor, even when a private entrepreneur, has been trained at a huge public expense not only in money, but in cooperation and good will from the public—in the form of donating their bodies for dissection and seeking care in hospitals and institutions where it is clearly understood that many of the physicians will be in training. Further, if the medical profession is to be anything more than "hired syringes" in performing euthanasia, physicians must develop their own independent rationale for the killing of terminally ill patients under their care. Simply accepting the patient's own declaration that his or her life has become an intolerable burden does not seem sufficient. There are virtually no external, objective grounds for establishing such an end point, as the Dutch experience attests.[84] The physician cannot euthanize a patient unless the physician's values and the patient's values coincide, which pushes the matter into the public arena. Further, it virtually mandates the development of guidelines or scenarios in which life "may not be worth living," in order to assist the physician's decision-making in individual cases—an extremely unhealthy and morally repugnant circumstance, in May's view.

The danger of establishing the right to euthanasia within the constitutionally protected right to privacy, as has been done with abortion in *Roe* v. *Wade,* worries some observers. A Supreme Court decision that swept away legislative prohibitions against euthanasia would have more far-reaching and immediate consequences than statewide, incremental initiatives, dangerous as these themselves may be. Further, once the right to end one's life has been extended as a matter of constitutional privacy, it would be difficult to draw the line at people suffering from imminently terminal illnesses. Euthanasia might extend to any suffering whatsoever, either physical or emotional, and whether immediately or remotely threatening.[85]

The experience in Holland makes it difficult to believe that government regulation will be particularly successful. Those who fear that once the door to euthanasia is opened, its practice will become rampant point to Holland with concern.

Of those Dutch patients who had their lives ended without their own express consent, an alarming 45 percent of their families were never even consulted. There were nearly five thousand reported cases of morphine overdoses in 1990, for example. Of those, 27 percent were done without a fully competent patient's knowledge, and 60 percent of practitioners failed to consult another physician before killing without the patient's consent. Further, the accurate cause of death was given on only one death certificate.[86] Physicians were equally noncompliant regarding the rules regulating voluntary euthanasia, failing to record the proceedings in writing (54%), not consulting another physician as required (19%), and concealing the fact that the patient died by euthanasia (72%).

In light of this legal and bureaucratic noncompliance, new regulations have been issued which encourage physician-assisted suicide in lieu of physician-administered euthanasia when possible; require that the consulting doctor not have a professional relationship with either the patient or the family; and guarantee that no physician be forced to perform euthanasia if such a treatment is against his or her principles. Such conscientious objectors, however, must so inform their patients and refer the patient to a physician who has no such objections.[87]

May quotes Leon Kass on the apparent inconsistency of holding that euthanasia is at once a private matter, yet still insisting on accurate governmental oversight. Kass, himself a physician, asks the rhetorical and somewhat cynical question:

> Must we, can we, should we, rely solely on the virtue of…unregulated medical practitioners—to protect the exposed and vulnerable lives of the infirm, the elderly, and the powerless who, incapable of real autonomy, will be deemed by others to have lives no longer worth living, or more likely worth sustaining at great medical expense?[88]

Carlos Gomez denies that the physician-patient relationship, even at the hour of death, is an essentially private one:

> [This overlooks] the public institutional quality of the profession of medicine…. For all its necessarily private and intimate aspects,…[medicine is] necessarily a public enterprise…. The claim to a right to death at the hands of a physician is essentially a private claim to a public good.[89]

Limits on Our Freedom

Catholic doctrine teaches that our human choices are limited by divine sovereignty. Though we are responsible for making informed health care decisions, there are limits to human freedom.

35

Life is a gift from God, and only God has control of its giving and taking. The principle of divine sovereignty asserts that God alone has absolute sovereignty over creation. Our stewardship over creation is limited: we share in God's dominion only as creatures. The restrictions placed on the first humans by God—as told in the creation stories and codified in the Ten Commandments—show that from the earliest times, the Bible has taught that human dominion over life, including our own, is limited. Aquinas asserted that we have the *use* of our lives, not their *possession*.[90] More recently John Paul II has argued against euthanasia by asserting our limited stewardship over life and death.[91]

Leaving the metaphysical and spiritual questions of stewardship aside, one view of why killing is wrong is that it robs the victim of a continued life or of a future valued for the fulfillment of plans and dreams. Accordingly, people have a moral right not to be killed. In ethicist Dan Brock's view, however, this right can be waived when a person comes to the determination that continued life is no longer desirable. Euthanasia, properly understood, is a case of waiving one's right not to be killed.

Brock allows that such a cavalier view of the rightness or wrongness of killing is not universally shared. He argues, however, that in a pluralistic society with separation of church and state, there is no place for arguments based on the religious view that all life comes from God. In his view, all arguments about inalienable rights are grounded in a belief in a supreme being.[92]

If euthanasia were licit, we would be able to honor the self-determination of those competent patients who wish it, but who cannot yet avail themselves of euthanasia because it is illegal. Besides benefiting that small minority of patients who would actually request euthanasia, its legalization would support the "right to choose" and permit euthanasia to be considered as an additional option of care near the end of life.[93] The legal availability of euthanasia would be a kind of "insurance policy" against being forced to endure life-saving procedures and techniques one does not desire. The fear of loss of control would then be minimized.

Dan Callahan maintains that the argument from self-determination is specious. If all that euthanasia proponents wanted was to be allowed to commit suicide, the debate would be far more limited. In the case of euthanasia, however, the matter is not that limited. The patient's self-determination can only be realized through the moral and physical assistance of another. Euthanasia is thus no longer a matter only of self-determination, but of a mutual social decision between two people: one, to be killed, and the other, to do the killing. Euthanasia is not a matter of self-determination. It is an act that requires two people to make it possible, and a complicit society to make it acceptable.[94]

Some might argue that a physician can simply assist in the suicide of his patient, or even actually perform euthanasia, by complying with the duty to honor the patient's wishes (we will consider the physician as an independent moral agent in chapter 8), but might the physician claim that he or she is simply cooperating in the moral agenda of the patient and thereby escape any moral credit or blame?

Formal cooperation requires that the will of the cooperator be the same as that of the principal actor; material cooperation makes no assumption. Thus, the physician may technically escape the charge of explicit formal cooperation by a declaration that his or her will is not at issue; the physician is merely honoring the will of the patient. Some ethicists would still charge the physician with *implicit* formal cooperation; by acting as the patient requests, the physician implicitly agrees with the patient's choice.

Even if the physician's will is different from the patient's, Catholic ethicists argue that directly aiding the patient's death is material cooperation and would still be wrong. Material cooperation, since it helps the principal actor perform an evil action but does not involve concurrence with the bad will, is wrong, but can be justified if proportionate reasons exist. More serious reasons are required when the cooperation is more closely involved in the act of the principle agent.[95]

Moral theologian James F. Keenan lists six questions that must be answered in every case of cooperation: (1) What is the object of A's activity? (2) Is A's cooperation in B's illicit activity formal or merely material? (3) Is the cooperation immediate or simply mediate? (4) Is the cooperation proximate or simply remote? (5) Does A have sufficient cause for acting? (6) Is A's cooperation indispensable?[96]

To speak of an *object* of an action that may have two or more effects is an important fundamental principle of classical Catholic moral theology. The object or act of administering pain medication to a dying patient for pain relief may have two effects: relieving pain and hastening death. The object is not intrinsically evil and thus is permitted as long as the intent is not to cause death, but rather to simply alleviate pain.

Moral theologian Richard M. Gula reviews the traditional Catholic three-fold moral analysis of an action: its *finis operantis,* the end or purpose of our action; its *finis operis,* the act-in-itself, that which could be objectively photographed; and the circumstances of the action. Actions that have the same material features (e.g., the administration of intravenous morphine to a terminal patient) can have different moral meanings, depending on the intentions that direct the actions. Moral actions are not, however, infinitely plastic. Certain actions, such as intentionally taking innocent human life, cannot be informed by even the best of intentions.[97]

Catholic teaching holds that the intrinsically evil nature of the action, along with its serious nature, forbids immediate material cooperation with euthanasia or physician-assisted suicide.[98]

Critics of the church's position would hold that the right to one's own life is inalienable. Not only can the individual not surrender this right, but he or she certainly cannot yield control over it to someone else. To put it another way, can our right to life—like our right to private property—be alienated if the price (happiness, relief of suffering) is right?

Those against euthanasia and physician-assisted suicide would insist that no cogent reasons have been brought forward to put the power to end a human life in someone else's hand, even or especially in the hands of physicians. Society has defined circumstances under which it is not permissible for adults to control the life of another, as in the case of slavery, or even to kill each other with mutual consent, as in the case of dueling. Both practices were eventually outlawed.

Further, this expansion in the permission to kill would come about just at a time when that right has become increasingly restricted in modern societies: Efforts to control the free flow of guns and arms, the abolition of capital punishment, and international rules for the conduct of war are examples.

In summary, self-determination fails because it usurps divine sovereignty, involves others in the decision (especially in euthanasia, but even in physician-assisted suicide), and is an attempt to alienate a fundamental human right, which society ought not tolerate. Patient choice can be so influenced by family, health care workers, economic, and other factors that the free nature of the choice is often suspect.

Chapter 4 ■
Compassion and Mercy toward the Dying

THE VERY TERM *MERCY KILLING* would suggest that one important motivation behind the euthanasia movement is mercy and compassion toward the dying. Many advocates of euthanasia assert that there is a significant number of cases in which even the best medical technology cannot alleviate the physical pain of the terminally ill. Moreover, our technological advances have done little or nothing to help ameliorate the psychological fear and existential anxiety experienced by all at the approach of death, more acutely by some than others. Indeed, the fear of being trapped on life-support machinery is clearly a new and modern fear. These advocates claim that we act out of compassionate concern for our fellow humans when we end their pointless suffering at their own request.[99]

Ethicist Dan Brock argues that euthanasia should be available as a compassionate means of ending the pain and suffering of those for whom the termination of life support or the refusal of aggressive treatment does not end their lives. Significant controversy surrounds the question of whether or not the fear of terminal pain and suffering underlie the entire demand for euthanasia and whether modern medicine is doing enough to eliminate such pain and suffering.

Most experts agree that in the vast majority of cases, pain and suffering can be minimized with proper application of medical technology; the fear that one will be forced to endure a lingering and painful death over which one has no control is not generally well founded. On the other hand, experts will also readily admit that in many cases, the care of the terminally ill is not optimal, and that there may be unnecessary pain and suffering at the end of life. There are many factors responsible for this. Physicians, even those who care for large numbers of terminally ill patients, have generally not been as well trained in alleviating pain and suffering as they have been in therapeutic intervention and diagnostic evaluation. Even the growth of the hospice movement has not seemed to affect the average practitioner of adult medicine. Some doctors have an unwarranted fear of causing addiction, even in terminal patients who require large doses of narcotics for pain control. In many states there are difficulties in dispensing and prescribing sufficient amounts of narcotics. Health care may not be available to groups of terminally ill patients for either financial or social reasons. Even those who argue for the availability of euthanasia realize that much more can be done to alleviate the pain and suffering of the dying.

Paradoxically, if adequate and expert care were available for all the dying, public support for euthanasia might diminish, perhaps significantly. Opponents feel that the fear of suffering a lingering painful death encourages a pro-euthanasia stand. In any case, proponents of euthanasia still argue that even with adequate end-of-life medical care, there would still be a need for euthanasia. They hold that in a select number of cases, the only compassionate and humane response to the intractable pain and suffering of a fellow human being is the merciful administration of euthanasia. Further, psychological pain and suffering is even less

41

well understood, and its treatment is generally far less successful by traditional medical and psychological means. They conclude that the more compassionate treatment for such patients is a quick and merciful end.

Many share the impression that those who die quickly of trauma or quietly in their sleep at a ripe old age have "good deaths." Thus, when we have it in our power to facilitate such "humane deaths," we fail in our obligations to our fellow beings when we do not do so.

This argument is straightforward, but problematic. The major impetus, at least in this country, for the legalization of euthanasia is focused on the right to self-determination. It does not follow, indeed it seems contradictory, to place the power of life and death in the hands of others, even if they act out of mercy and compassion. Acting "mercifully"—without clear and certain direction from an incompetent patient, as some who advocate euthanasia would do—violates the ideal of self-determination.

Opponents of euthanasia argue that its proponents generally restrict their support for euthanasia to individuals who voluntarily request it. Having garnered support for these limited cases, they almost always move on to discuss *involuntary* euthanasia for those who are unable to request it. Relief of suffering becomes one of the primary motivations for acting in this way. There is an extremely unhealthy coupling of the autonomy/mercy arguments.

Critics of the "merciful ending" interpretation claim that a society cannot weigh in at the end of someone's life with a kinder, gentler way out when it has "starved the aged and dying [of] compassion for many of their declining years."[100] A country must earn the moral option to kill for mercy by supporting the *lives* of its citizens with compassion and mercy.

It is feared that the option of euthanasia may become the only realistic alternative offered to a significant proportion of the elderly and dying. The society kills out of "convenience, not compassion," opines one anti-euthanasia ethicist. The compassion of a society must be visible throughout its social fabric, not just as life unravels at is edges.

William F. May is a severe critic of the argument for euthanasia from compassion. He fears that active euthanasia might become a "final solution for handling the problem of the aged poor."[101] As a greater proportion of our society ages and strains the already insufficient social security and welfare systems, this issue will become one of critical concern. He feels that the true test of a compassionate society lies not in investing even more money in acute-care facilities, but in shifting our medical priorities to preventative, rehabilitative, long-term, and terminal care health services, which would provide all patients with a realistic alternative to a quick death.

May is not sanguine that reasonable alternatives for the aged and aging will quell the discussion on euthanasia altogether. The Netherlands, after all, has more comprehensive health care coverage than the United States, but also a court-sanctioned euthanasia program. Nevertheless, the onus to provide adequate health care for our aging and dying citizens remains. Our social covenant obligates us to "provide care always."[102] Most of the time, this will involve the obligation to treat, but at some point, treatment may not serve the patient's best interests. Even at such a point, our social covenant obliges us to continue to care. Indeed, unceasing care is the assumption that undergirds the morally permissible action of allowing to die. The licitness of passive euthanasia depends upon the degree to which the act of letting die is supported by the covenantal obligation to care.[103]

May wishes to ensure that if prohibitions against active euthanasia and assisted suicide remain in place, there be even more safeguards against abandoning those who are being allowed to die in pain. As efforts to treat are relinquished, "efforts to care for, make comfortable and console must intensify."[104] The U.S.

Catholic bishops, in their *Ethical and Religious Directives for Catholic Health Care Services,* remind physicians that "the task of medicine is to care even when it cannot cure."[105]

Many issues that have traditionally been seen as "nursing care" of the terminally ill need more research and attentive clinical application: effective pharmacologic control of pain; managing end-stage gastrointestinal, respiratory, and agonal symptoms; treating skin problems and pressure ulcers; fever; weakness; and maintaining mental alertness as much as possible or desirable. Better training of the general internist in these areas could help bring symptomatic relief to many more dying patients. Medical research has not sufficiently addressed the needs of the terminally ill and dying. An expert physician in hospice care observed: "Often it is easier to get a heart transplant or cataract surgery than supper or a back rub, let alone effective pain relief."[106] Studies have shown that primary care physicians who care for the dying routinely underdiagnose depression and undermedicate for pain.[107]

Opponents of euthanasia maintain that our compassion for the pain and suffering of the dying should cause us to redouble our efforts to improve the quality and distribution of health care for the terminally ill. Supporters of euthanasia claim that this is insufficient. In their view, true compassion consists in helping the patient escape his or her misery with an easy, painless death.

Chapter 5 ■
Killing vs. Allowing to Die

THIS IS AN EXTREMELY IMPORTANT DISTINCTION in the euthanasia debate. Generally speaking, opponents of euthanasia maintain that there is a clear moral distinction between merely allowing to die and actually causing or deliberately hastening someone's death. For some it is a crucial moral discernment; for others, it represents either casuistry or moral fiction.

Ethicists Dan Brock and John Fletcher find no significant distinction between allowing to die and killing.[108] Brock asserts that euthanasia is already practiced on a large scale. Some argue that physicians should not participate in euthanasia since there are sacrosanct prohibitions against physicians killing—"nothing in the currently accepted practice of medicine is deliberate killing."[109] But Brock makes the case that physicians already kill, because he sees no moral distinction between allowing to die and killing outright. Attempting to maintain a distinction between killing and allowing to die is moral legerdemain, in his view.

He illustrates his point by citing the case of an alert, competent, respirator-dependent patient with ALS who repeatedly requests to be removed from the respirator and thereby allowed to die. Many reasonable people would agree that the physician should comply with the patient's request. This is viewed as "allowing to die," not a deliberate act of medical homicide. He compares the physician's external actions with those of a greedy son impatient for his inheritance who removes his mother from the respirator while no one is attending her. Brock claims that both the doctor and the greedy son have killed. Admittedly, the doctor has done so with the consent of the patient, acting with the good intention to honor the patient's wishes, in the role of a physician who is socially authorized to carry out the wishes of the patient. The son acts from selfish motivation and with neither the authorization of his mother nor of society. Nonetheless, Brock claims that these important distinctions do not necessarily show that the son killed while the physician merely allowed to die. Both killing and allowing to die can be done with or without our consent and either within or outside of a socially sanctioned role authorizing one to do so.[110]

Withdrawing medical treatment has been seen as merely standing aside and refusing to block the natural consequences of a fatal disease. Brock says that the son cannot be construed to have killed when his actions lead to the very same end as the compassionate family and physician. He argues that physicians who claim they are not killing their patients when they remove them from respirators are just refusing to face reality. Since society does not view physicians as killers, when they remove life support equipment from patients their actions must not, cannot be interpreted as murder. According to Brock, we ought to reject the view that all killing is unjustifiable, not that physicians should not or do not kill. Some killings are justified, including some instances of stopping life support.[111] Brock does not enumerate other "justified killings," but for some at least, they might include self-defense, capital punishment, and just war.

Brock proposes that attributing the patient's death to the inevitable progress of the disease, standing aside and "letting nature take its course," is psychologically distancing language that comforts physicians and family alike. It falsely allows them to limit their moral responsibility for the patient's death. The more correct moral analysis, in Brock's view, is that they do bear responsibility for killing the patient; it is the patient's consent to allow life support to be withdrawn that limits the physician's and family's responsibility for the patient's death.[112]

Fletcher also maintains that the distinction between active and passive euthanasia is "worn out." We have maintained this moral fiction, he says, because fatal actions appear worse than fatal omissions. But exceptions can be imagined in each category. Some actions that lead to death are acceptable. He cites the administration of a large dose of morphine intended to relieve pain, which, as an unintended and secondary effect, hastens or causes the patient's death.[113] On the other hand, omissions may be equally grave as commissions. It would be wrong to fail to treat a healthy elderly patient's pneumonia, for example. The moral justification in each case depends not on an active/passive, omission/commission distinction, but rather upon the motives and intent of the moral agent(s).

May disagrees with Fletcher's arguments. The exceptions to a boundary crossing rule do not of themselves argue against respecting the boundary at all. Society draws all kinds of lines: minimum ages for drivers' licenses, voting, social security benefits, and so on. Further, nature itself supplies a boundary line between natural and human agency. In allowing to die, the physician, the nurse, and the family "simply step out of the way" to let disease and other natural forces bring a life to its natural end. In active euthanasia and assisted suicide, a human being does the killing. There is no confusing the two. Even if the human motive in both cases is compassion, there remains an important difference between letting the patient die and killing the patient.[114]

Ethicist Dan Maguire discusses the omission/commission

47

problem with sensitivity and insight. What is the moral difference between killing and allowing to die? Is there guilt by omission? He tells the story of a woman who was legally convicted for failing to prevent the death by suicide of her husband, who hung himself before her in a fit of rage at the conclusion of an argument. She omitted the performance of any actions that would have saved his life.[115] Most physicians would accept a distinction between failing to act medically and intervening directly to kill a patient. Even when the result is the same—death—it seems easier to justify omission rather than commission.

Some (like Joseph Fletcher) see no moral distinction between omission and commission regarding mercy killing. In their view, the distinction is a cloudy one, since the decision either to withhold medical treatment or to administer a fatal medication has the same result and, in fact, the same intention. "A decision not to keep a patient alive is as morally deliberate as a decision to end a life."[116]

Simply because acts of omission and commission are both deliberate and have the same result does not confer moral equivalence, in Maguire's view. They differ in their effects. There is a difference to caregivers and family alike between failing to administer antibiotics for pneumonia in a terminal case and administering a fatal dose of morphine. Death, even when forestalled by appropriate and aggressive medical treatment, can bring on feelings of guilt in the survivors. The administration of a fatal medication would certainly compound their misgivings and guilt. A lingering and painful death, however, may also foster feelings of guilt for not having expedited death and helped to alleviate some of the suffering.

For almost all physicians, even those in favor of euthanasia, it would be easier to stop supportive or resuscitative measures than to administer or order a deadly injection.[117] Even if the cessation of medical treatment would bring about death as quickly as administration of a fatal drug, the physician who disconnects a respirator can feel as though he or she merely let the disease advance, or let death have its way. Maguire carefully notes that this does not mean that deliberate termination of a life could not be moral, only that most physicians would understand you if you said that omission and commission are not the same thing in cases of euthanasia.[118]

Omission and commission also differ in their effects on society. The projected impact is greatest for those who subscribe to the "wedge theory," which holds that allowing any cases of euthanasia or assisted suicide could set off a chain reaction of unforeseen and disastrous consequences. (See chapter 7 where the wedge theory, or slippery slope argument, will be discussed in more detail.) But even those who justify certain cases of euthanasia must admit that death by commission gives more control to the one who dispenses the death, and might be abused for tax or inheritance purposes or for other ulterior motives.

Maguire notes that both actions may differ in their deliberateness. Omission may result from a kind of moral paralysis. It can be the result of the inability to overcome nonvolitional forces like the drag of moral acedia or confusion. While *not to decide* may also be *to decide,* it must also be admitted that sometimes it truly is "not to decide."

Omissions may, however, be fully deliberate and decisive acts. The decision not to operate on a child, for example, can be a painful decision reached after grave consideration. It is not, however, the same psychological act that moves you to give a child a fatal injection. Either act may be immoral or moral (according to Maguire), but they are not the same, and the distinctions may be crucial. The administration of a fatal dose of medication has a finality to it that failure to operate does not have. It closes off life and bars any other alternatives. For this reason, such a decision must be surrounded by even more serious deliberateness and moral analysis.

Moral agency is more diffuse in cases of omission. It is easier to say who did something than to say who did not do something. If what was omitted should have been done (at least in someone's view), then it is difficult to determine who is most responsible for the omission, since, literally, *everyone* did not do it.

Finally, omission and commission take on different forms. Each can be specific and each may be moral or immoral, but not by virtue of belonging to a specific category. Maguire gives some examples of acts of omission: not steering a rolling car away from a child in its path; not stopping to tackle an armed robber; not giving insulin to an otherwise healthy diabetic; not giving morphine to a terminal cancer patient in pain; not attending to a terminal patient after all medication has been stopped. Each omission is different and needs to be subjected to ethical analysis and examination.[119]

Analyzing the action itself, the intention of the one performing it, and the circumstances in which it is carried out is oftentimes difficult. How can we reconcile the occasionally evil effects of actions which were meant to acheive good? Can we ever perform an evil act to achieve a great good? Catholic moral theologians have developed the Principle of Double Effect in an attempt to wrestle with these questions.

The Principle of Double Effect

This is a time-honored principle in Catholic moral theology. It accepts the fact that most of our actions in this world have mixed outcomes, both good and bad. While it is never acceptable to directly will or perform an evil, there are circumstances where an unintended evil may be a tolerable and predictable outcome of some action deliberately taken for a proportionately greater good. Even though the use of narcotic analgesics for pain management in the terminally ill may produce coma or cardiovascular compromise and hasten a patient's death, these are unintentional effects. The intended effect is the compassionate relief of the patient's pain and suffering. The action taken has unintended side-effects.

A framework has been developed to help assess the morality of an action using the principle of double effect. The four classic criteria an action must meet before being considered morally acceptable are[120]:

1. The action itself is good or indifferent. Baseline implication: there are intrinsically immoral acts.
2. The good effect is not brought about by the evil. Evil cannot be used to achieve good: the end does not justify the means.
3. The evil effect is not directly intended. This is tricky. There are many difficulties: How does one determine one's "intentions"? Are intentions what makes for the morality of an action? Isn't a moral agent responsible for all the effects of an action, intended or not?
4. A proportionate reason admits causing or tolerating the evil effect.

Closely linked with the distinction of the double effect is the opinion held by Catholic moral philosophers that, given acceptable circumstances, discontinuing a treatment is the moral equivalent of not having initiated it. One may, for instance, intubate a patient and place him or her on a respirator in the hope of recovery. If there is no improvement in the patient's condition, the respirator may be removed. Removing the respirator is the moral equivalent of not having intubated the patient in the first place, whether due to more medical caution, the existence of advance directives or a surrogate's decision, or perhaps to the use of superior diagnostic or prognostic skill (making the clinical assessment that the medical intervention was likely to be useless).

The Congregation for the Doctrine of the Faith's *Declaration on Euthanasia* states that it is "also permitted, with the patient's consent, to interrupt these means [the means of life support provided by the most advanced medical techniques, even experimental ones], where the results fall short of expectations."[121]

Many clinicians, however, would find it difficult to discontinue what is at least in some sense a successful treatment, for example, the patient's mechanical ventilation once it has been initiated. Extubating a respirator-dependent patient may seem to many the same as killing the patient. Maguire's careful discussion of the distinction between omission and commission helps here, but more clarification is needed on this issue.

This important area of argumentation needs summation. The distinction between allowing to die and killing is crucial. It must be determined not solely by outcome or by an analysis of the external act(s). "Euthanasia's terms of reference, therefore, are to be found in the intention of the will and in the methods used."[122] The principle of double effect can be of salutary benefit in helping to analyze individual situations, keeping in mind that refusal to begin excessively burdensome treatments and the withdrawal of such treatments are equally morally acceptable.

Nutrition and Hydration

This a troublesome area in medical ethics and can only be discussed briefly here. Many feel that nutrition and hydration, even when medically administered through feeding tubes or intravenous lines, occupy a special place in the care of the terminally ill. Since they are the baseline requirements for life, and since they generally can be administered without extraordinary expense and without significant discomfort to the patient, many feel that nutrition and hydration must always be provided. They do not find that the permanently unconscious patient is necessarily dying or suffering from a terminal condition; for them, failure to provide food and hydration is slowly starving to death someone whose life we have determined is not worth sustaining.[123]

Others see the illness that produces the inability to eat or take fluids as a fatal disease. The intervention of physicians and caregivers to provide nutrition and hydration actually protracts the course of the illness. In this view, nutrition and hydration is viewed as any other medical treatment and can therefore be stopped when its burdens outweigh the potential benefits. Ceasing to provide nutrition and hydration may simply be another way of letting a patient die, but does not necessarily directly intend to kill the patient.

Magisterial documents differ in the degree to which they embrace one or the other of these positions. Statements issued by the bishops of Texas and by Cardinal Bernardin take the position that nutrition and hydration are medical treatments subject to basically the same contingencies as all other treatments, including the burdens/benefits analysis. The bishops of Florida, Pennsylvania, and New Jersey have taken a more conservative approach, considering nutrition and hydration as a basic human need, not a medical treatment.

Whether one views nutrition and hydration as either human care or medical treatment has important implications for the killing vs. letting die distinction. For some, failing to provide adequate nutrition or hydration is tantamount to killing a patient, while for others it would simply be letting the patient die. Critics who contend that there is no distinction at all (like Brock, who nevertheless believes that the "killing" is justifiable; or like the vitalists who insist on using all available treatments) can only point to the conflicting statements of the Catholic bishop's conferences with puzzlement.

A statement made by Cardinal Bernardin in 1988 shows great pastoral wisdom in attempting to come to a more unified position on the hydration/nutrition issue:

> I am convinced that from a moral point of view the essential bond between food, water, and life argues convincingly for the presumption that nutrition and hydration should always be provided. But I am also convinced that we are not morally obliged to do everything that is technically possible. In other words, there are cases where we would not be obliged artificially to provide nutrition and hydration. The challenge is to develop a nuanced public policy to protect against an attitude that could erode respect for the inviolable dignity of human life. If we do not resolve this critical issue *in a way that resonates with the common sense of people of good will,* then we may contribute to the sense of desperation that will lead people to consider euthanasia as an alternative solution to the problem.[124] (emphasis mine)

In 1995, the NCCB document *Ethical and Religious Directives for Catholic Health Care Services* summarized the current state of the question among the American bishops and also emphasized the points of already widespread agreement. All state Catholic conferences and individual bishops agree that hydration and nutrition are not morally obligatory when they either bring no comfort to a person who is imminently dying or when they cannot be assimilated by a person's body. The directive states that "there should be a presumption in favor of providing nutrition and hydration to all patients, including patients who require medically assisted nutrition and hydration, as long as this is of sufficient benefit to outweigh the burdens involved to the patient."[125] The document further notes that the morality of withdrawing medically assisted hydration and nutrition from a person who is in the condition recognized by physicians as the persistent vegetative state (PVS) requires "further reflection."[126]

Judicial decisions may further blur the distinction in some minds between killing and allowing to die. Ethicist James Bresnahan cites two cases before the U.S. Supreme Court that will have a major impact on how the legal distinction between these two actions can be maintained. The first, a case in California, asserts that since patients have a right to refuse life-sustaining treatments, including food and water, they have a right to hasten their own deaths. By that fact, legislation prohibiting physician-assisted suicide is unconstitutional. A second case in New York found that since patients on artificial life support had a right to hasten their deaths by requesting that their physicians remove such equipment, others who are terminally ill but not on life support are discriminated against. They too, should be able to hasten their deaths if they so desire, by asking their physicians to prescribe medications to accomplish it. Both cases have conflated refusal of treatment with the hastening of dying, and have begun to blur the distinction between what some call passive and active euthanasia. While the complex legal issues involved are beyond the scope of this discussion, the Supreme Court cases point out the treacherous ground between killing and allowing to die.[127]

Theological and philosophical discussion will continue about the distinctions between killing and allowing to die. For Catholic ethicists and others, the distinction is crucial. For others, it is moral nit picking. Both our understanding of human disease and death and our view of human moral agency influence our stance on this important issue.

Chapter 6 ■
The Principle of the Common Good

LIVING IN HUMAN SOCIETY places limits on our freedom. We are born into social relationships, raised in them, nurtured in them, frustrated in them.[124] There is virtually no way a person can live and escape social relationships, even if one so desired. Catholic teaching insists that social structures must be ordered to support the dignity of each person. Even private acts have public and social consequences. How we die certainly affects others.

The principle of the common good makes it important to judge the effects of our actions on others. The common good has been an important part of Catholic social justice teaching, yet many might more likely think it an American democratic innovation. Even though the common good respects and serves the interests of individual persons, which distinguishes it from Marxism, the common good ultimately upholds the collective good as more important than the good of any one individual.

It believes, however, that the society will flourish only if the individual flourishes as well. As one ethicist sums up, "To seek the common good, then, is to seek those actions and policies that would contribute to the total well-being of individual persons and the community."[129] Occasionally, however, the freedom of the individual may be frustrated vis-à-vis society. The example of traffic signals can be used. The common good demands that we regulate the flow of traffic in our cities; thus we install traffic lights. Even though these traffic control signals frustrate our ability to travel as unencumbered as we might like, they structure and promote the public order.

One of the difficulties with appealing to the common good in our society is that American culture can be envisioned as a loose amalgamation of separate and diverse groups with few if any interests, goals, or dreams in common. In contrast, the common good is an idea bound up with the virtue of solidarity and social justice. It views society as a complex, organic entity, not merely a confederation of civic associations. The American emphasis on the sharp distinction between public and private, and on the rights of the individual—especially the right of the individual to choose—makes it difficult to see a common good.[130] The principle of the common good as applied to death argues that no death in our society is truly "private." How one person dies affects us all.

The common good argument is a countervailing balance to the self-determination argument: certainly the Catholic position holds these two values in creative tension. Many would argue that it is the task of American democracy to strike a creative balance between autonomy and the common good as well.

The principle of the common good goes beyond the arguments adduced for placing limits on self-determination, and calls us to consider the impact that allowing euthanasia might have on our general attitude toward preserving life and the taking of life. We have considered some of these: Will euthanasia be used as a cost-saving measure to avoid expensive long-term disability care? Or as an easy fix to the complex problems of aging and disability? Might it encourage funds to be siphoned away from medical research for the aging, or from hospice or long-term rehabilitation facilities? Would the very existence of euthanasia as a legal, realistic choice force the aged to "justify" their existence? These questions and others have no easy answers. The common good argument makes the case that our lives and decisions influence others in complex, interconnected ways.

Catholic social teaching rejects the notion of the rugged American individual yet still holds that each individual must be fully able to participate in his or her own perfection. It views the human person as social by nature. It views the public order as consisting of three major elements, which the state has the responsibility to provide: justice, public peace, and public morality. The government does not bear full responsibility for providing for the common good, however. The individual citizen also bears a responsibility by means of meaningful participation in government and by volunteer activity, especially in those areas in which governmental activity may be either deficient or not desirable. Moreover, the common good stretches across the boundaries of nation-states and cultures and embraces the entire human family. An evolving global awareness can be traced through the papal encyclicals *Pacem in terris, Populorum progressio,* and *Sollicitudo rei socialis,* indicating an increasing awareness by John XXIII, Paul VI, and John Paul II of the interdependence of the global human community.

The Christian dimensions of the common good are expressed as the virtue of solidarity—a firm and persevering determination to commit oneself to the common good. It is the recognition that we have all been born into a single human family: all that we have has been given to us in trust for the benefit of all. If we accept God's unconditional love for each person, we see that human solidarity has to be universal. Solidarity emphasizes our human interdependence and calls for collaboration in all our efforts. It transforms our interpersonal relationships and must be exercised not only by individuals, but by entire nations as well.

Solidarity helps us to see the other as neighbor and helper, and condemns any instrumental use of persons.[131]

It decries euthanasia as the ultimate abandonment of the terminally ill by his or her human family. Even if carried out between a consenting patient and a willing physician, euthanasia or physician-assisted suicide would have far-reaching consequences. It would thicken the already threatening matrix of social sin.

Pro-euthansia advocates also appeal to the common good argument to make their case. Euthanasia or physician-assisted suicide might help reduce the high costs of medical care for the terminally ill and make new financial resources available for purposes that might better serve the common good (for example childhood immunization programs). Those in favor of legalized euthanasia or physician-assisted suicide have cautiously limited their use of the common good argument to economic grounds— how should we best spend our limited resources in caring for our community? This may be in part due to the Nazis' broad use of the common good argument on social and eugenic grounds: the debilitated, the elderly and the genetically inferior were eleminated for the good of the *volk*. Even so, some ethicists have begun speculating about the possibility that we may each have a "duty to die," which considers not only the economic health of our family and community, but also the family's emotional well-being.[132]

Chapter 7 ■
The Slippery Slope Argument

IN A PLURALISTIC SOCIETY where the Christian absolute prohibition against the taking of innocent life may not be accepted on religious grounds,[133] the slippery slope argument can be helpful in preventing the legalization of objectionable exceptions to legal statutes prohibiting euthanasia or physician-assisted suicide. Opponents of euthanasia maintain that not only is the argument persuasive in its theoretical form, but that actual evidence from Nazi Germany and the contemporary Netherlands supports it.

The Generic Slippery Slope Argument

The slippery slope argument against any thesis is difficult to evaluate. Often, the argument must be made from a theoretical position only, since it is commonly posed against a potentially dangerous situation that does not yet exist. In the case of euthanasia, proponents of the slippery slope argument claim that the experience with state-run euthanasia in Nazi Germany, contemporary judicial and medical policy in the Netherlands, and American abortion policy in the wake of *Roe* v. *Wade*[134] instantiate the theoretical argument. We shall examine the circumstances in Nazi Germany and the contemporary Netherlands after looking at the theoretical applicability of the argument.

Slippery slope arguments arise in many areas of practical ethics. Someone is sure to raise the objection: But if we allow *this,* then how will we prevent *that?* And since *that* is unacceptable, *this* should not be permitted either. The argument carries many aliases: thin edge of the wedge, allowing the camel's nose into the tent, the domino theory, the tip of the iceberg, the primrose path, and, most commonly used, the slippery slope. Once you take the first step, relentless descent to the awful bottom follows.[135]

There are really at least two forms of the argument: the psychological form and the logical form. The psychological argument claims that if an exception is made to a traditional rule, there will be a tendency for unwarranted exceptions to follow. The logical form of the argument speaks to the grounds available for denying any further exceptions to the rule. If we allow *this,* then we have no rational grounds for not allowing *that.*[136]

Recently David Lamb has offered a refinement of the logical form of the argument. It is not that one can no longer distinguish between the morality of the wanted from the unwanted exception. There is a world of moral difference, he points out, between a case of requested euthanasia and a case of forced euthanasia. The problem is the move from an absolute prohibition against killing to exceptions based on such concepts as voluntariness, intractable pain, or terminal illness. In moving from an absolute rule, one moves from determinate concepts and descriptions to loose concepts and "definitions and determinations [that] are inherently arbitrary."[137]

Lamb illustrates his theoretical point with an argument that refers to the justifications given for euthanasia. Once the objections leave the "sanctity of life" ethic, which would prohibit all cases of euthanasia, to a "quality of life" ethic, which would permit at least some, the concepts move from absolute rules to concepts that are "unlikely to provide an unequivocal guide for our action."[138]

Since the mistake of killing someone who would be better off alive is worse, in his view, than the mistake of leaving someone alive who is better off dead, Lamb believes that the slippery slope argument does, in theory, justify maintaining the absolute prohibition against even voluntary euthanasia.[139]

Critics of this position argue that Lamb has not sufficiently argued his case. They contend that (1) since he makes exceptions to the absolute prohibition against killing to allow killing in self-defense, he must necessarily use the ambiguous language of "reasonable fear," "grave harm," etc.; (2) though a wrongful euthanasia "permanently removes all options," while the person wrongfully left alive still has options, it is not automatically evident that the survivor's fate of prolonged suffering, incapacity, and so forth, is "better"; and (3) there is no escape from the moral necessity of applying even the most absolute of rules; no rule is self-applying.[140]

Ethicists Tom L. Beauchamp and James F. Childress discuss the logical form of the slippery slope argument against mercy killing under the general principle of nonmaleficence, or doing no harm. They conclude that it does not offer "a clear and compelling reason to oppose mercy killing."[141] Relevant distinctions between what must be accepted as a general practice and what can be tolerated as an occasional act can be drawn; we are not subject to uncontrollable implications from general principles.[142] They do, however, find the psychological/sociological form of the argument persuasive, as we will see below.

Critics of the slippery slope argument consider it an argument of last resort used by defenders of the status quo. Some who accept the logical form of the slippery slope argument admit that the case against their position does allow exceptions, but insist that if these few reasonable exceptions are permitted, it would be difficult or impossible to prohibit other exceptions. Their critics insist that they cannot concede the argument to their opponents on logical grounds and so shift the grounds of the debate to the psychological/sociological version of the argument.

Dan Brock argues that "opponents of voluntary euthanasia on slippery slope grounds have not provided the data or evidence necessary to turn their speculative concerns into well grounded likelihoods."[143] Brock outlines four procedural safeguards that he maintains will "substantially reduce, but not eliminate the potential for abuse of a policy permitting voluntary active euthanasia." He illustrates what might be a logically defensible attack against any slippery slope argument by denying any intrinsic connection between the exception and its rule and proposing that strict regulations will disallow undesirable, broad-ranging exemptions from the rule. His critics, however, counter that it is not realistic to neutralize each objection by assuring the worriers about the slippery slope that abuses can be prevented, and that wise and rational decisions can be made by all.

There may be no grounds for settling the logical slippery slope argument, but the psychological and sociological forms of the argument carry a certain force. The psychological/sociological version examines the society and culture, specifically the impact of making exceptions to rules or changing the rules in a more permissive direction. If certain restraints against killing are removed, a moral decline might result because various psychological or social forces make it unlikely that people will draw distinctions that are, in principle, clear and defensible. Childress and Beauchamp offer a helpful analogy. The rules against killing in a society are not isolated fragments; they are threads in a fabric of rules, drawn in part from nonmaleficence, which support respect for human life. The more threads we remove, the weaker the fabric becomes. If we focus on attitudes and not merely rules, the general attitude of respect for life may be eroded by shifts in particular areas.[144]

There are at least two actual instances to consider in the case of euthanasia: the historical slippery slope of medical ethics in Germany before World War II and the current medical ethics in the Netherlands.

Nazi Germany

There is a reluctance to discuss the Nazi experience with euthanasia. This may be attributable to several reasons. Until recently, very little scholarly literature on the subject existed.[145] In addition, there may be some hesitation to discuss so-called Nazi ethics. Some fear that even discussing the ethical rationale used by the Nazis for their policies and experiments might confer some legitimacy on them.

It is also difficult for scientists to examine critically what happened during the Nazi years because of the extensive complicity and responsibility of the medical and scientific communities for the Nazi atrocities. The racism that flourished in Nazi Germany found widespread support from biology and medicine. The horrible consequences of the Final Solution were administered by doctors and healers. Science, as we will see, permeated the Holocaust: from designing and running the gas chambers and crematoria to operating the transportation network and selecting those who would die based on psychological, physical, or anthropological criteria.

Use of the Nazi analogy leaves one somewhat unsure of how to respond. Comparing attitudes or behavior in contemporary medicine with the Nazis is dangerous. For one thing, many simply cannot make the judgment as to whether or not the comparison is legitimate, and if so, what the implications of this might be. Author Arthur Caplan believes that while wholesale charges of Nazism are unwarranted and difficult to evaluate, there are some areas in which enough information about the Nazis is available to make cautious comparisons and informed judgments.[146]

Simply showing, for example, that the Nazis permitted and encouraged euthanasia does not itself show that there is any similarity between these events and occurrences of euthanasia today. In fact, adequate information may lead to the conclusion that the Nazi analogy does not hold. One such example, Caplan believes, is the termination of treatment, an issue central to such American cases as Quinlan, Cruzan, and others. Just because their next of kin decided for one reason or another not to provide food or to terminate their medical treatment, this does not make them Nazis.[147]

A brief history of the use of euthanasia in Nazi Germany can make any comparisons made between then and now more precise. Three main programs formed the heart of the Nazi program of medicalized "racial cleansing": the sterilization law, the Nuremberg Laws, and the euthanasia operation. Many feel that these programs, especially euthanasia, cleared the path for subsequent mass killings.[148]

The 1933 Sterilization Law permitted the forcible sterilization of those suffering from "genetically determined" diseases, such as feeblemindedness, schizophrenia, manic-depressive insanity, genetic epilepsy, Huntington's chorea, genetic blindness, deafness, and severe alcoholism. It was drafted with the help of leading German social scientists.[149]

Genetic Health Courts and Appellate Genetic Health Courts were set up in 1934 to help adjudicate the sterilizations. These courts were adjuncts to the local civil court and were usually presided over by two doctors and a lawyer. One of the three had to be an expert on "genetic pathology." Physicians were required to report and register every case of genetic illness known to them.[150]

It is estimated that up to four hundred thousand Germans were sterilized. Medical supply companies (such as Schering, now Schering-Plough) manufactured the necessary equipment, and medical student dissertations on sterilization techniques, consequences, and so on proliferated. At the same time, abortions for healthy German women were declared illegal, while sometimes being forced on other "inferior" genetic stock.[151] Access to birth control was also severely curtailed, except, of course, for Jews.

The Nuremberg laws (promulgated by Hitler in 1935) excluded Jews from citizenship and forbade marriage and sexual relations between Jews and non-Jews. The Marital Health Law required couples to submit to medical examinations before marriage to prevent possible "racial pollution." The Nuremberg Code was considered a public health code and was administered primarily by physicians. Enforcement of the Marital Health Exams fell to the Public Health Offices, established throughout Germany by 1935.[152]

In October 1939, just one month after World War II began, Hitler issued orders that certain doctors were to be commissioned to grant a mercy death (*Gnadentod*) to patients judged to be incurably sick by medical examination.

Reich Leader Bouhler and Dr. Brandt are charged with the responsibility for expanding the authority of physicians, to be designated by name, to the end that patients considered incurable according to the best available human judgment of their state of health can be granted a mercy death.[153]

By August 1941, more than seventy thousand "incurable" patients from German mental hospitals had been gassed.

The main justification initially given for the gassings was

economic: to free up necessary hospital beds for the war wounded. The first gassings of mental patients occurred in Posen, in Poland, on October 15, 1939. By August 1941, involuntary euthanasia had become part of normal hospital routine: handicapped infants were regularly put to death; and adults who required long-term psychiatric care or extensive nursing care, such as the elderly, were being killed in an operation code named "T4" for the address of the Chancellery office at Tiergarten from which the operation was coordinated.[154]

Under T4 policy, a doctor had to do the actual killing in accord with the motto of Dr. Viktor Brack, head of the project: "The syringe belongs in the hand of a physician."[155] All the killings—eventually done by gassings after lethal injections had been tried and discarded as too time consuming—were supervised by physicians.

Secrecy and cover-up for this operation included issuing false death certificates and registries to make the final cause of death correspond in some way to the patient's condition prior to gassing. The nature of the procedure itself was camouflaged from the patients, who were led in groups to the gas chambers, designed to appear like showers.[156]

Lufton and others draw a direct link between the already smoothly functioning T4 killing project and the initiation of the Final Solution, the extermination of the Jews. Even before the mass extermination of Jews, Jewish inmates of institutions in Germany already were exempt from the usual criteria for T4 extermination (mental deficiency, schizophrenia, inability to maintain employment, and so forth). For them "no special consultations or discussions...were necessary."[157]

In August of 1941, Clemens Count von Galen, the Catholic bishop of Münster, gave a heroic homily denouncing the gassings and filed formal charges against any deportations. Galen said, "We wish to withdraw ourselves and our faithful from their [the

Nazi authorities] influence, so that we may not be contaminated by their thinking and ungodly behavior, so that we may not participate and share with them in the punishment which a just God should and will pronounce upon all those who—like ungrateful Jerusalem—do not wish what God wishes."[158]

Partly due to Galen's preaching and partly due to protests by German citizens after details of the hospital gassings had become public, the gas chambers, "which had become standard equipment at the large psychiatric hospitals, were dismantled and shipped east to Majdanek, Auschwitz, and Treblinka. Doctors, nurses, and technicians often followed the equipment. The killing machinery provided a continuity between the 'lives not worth living' in German mental hospitals and the destruction of ethnic and social minorities."[159]

Recent works document the chilling details of the complicity of the medical profession in the Nazi extermination programs and in the gruesome medical experimentation that went on throughout the war using camp inmates as guinea pigs.[160]

As we learn more about Nazi eugenics, euthanasia, and extermination programs, what relevance might this have for our euthanasia debate?

Lisa Sowle Cahill asserts that the task of those who confront the medical horrors of the Holocaust is neither to trivialize nor demonize the Nazi experience.

She draws several lessons:

1. *"Listen."* The survivors are the only ones who in the truest sense can understand the Holocaust. Cahill warns against trying to harness the "lessons" of the Holocaust for our own political or religious purposes; this only objectifies the Holocaust victims once again. The temptation to overreach for the Nazi analogy on any number of human rights issues like abortion, embryo research, or euthanasia can be strong.

2. *"Application of our listening must be nuanced and careful."*
Cahill urges that we carefully examine the causes and motivations of behaviors, including medical procedures and
techniques. It was distinctive of Jews under the Nazi regime
to be marked for extinction and to be treated in this way by
the scientific community. We should be careful that apparent similarities in policy or circumstances have the same
sorts of *causes* before we can truly know how to proceed.

She urges caution not only in regard to causes, but also in
results. Will a similar chain of reactions result? Can a
wartime German slippery slope predict another? Where
might similar idolatry cause a blind spot in the American
analysis? Few would suggest that a medically arranged
Holocaust is likely, or even in part due to the sad history of
World War II, but the hegemony of economics in the United
States might parallel the German obsession with medicine
and science at the start of World War II. People marginal-
ized by unemployment and underinsurance might be suit-
able victims for our society's cruelty or scapegoating. Our
moral vision may have its eyeballs peeled for the appear-
ance of another Hitler, but we may be relatively blind to the
moral evil lurking quietly in the background.

3. *"The danger in a pluralistic society of moral nihilism or
lack of agreed upon ethical principles is ever present."* As
Cahill notes, we seem to lack confidence that we can arrive
at agreement on any of the crucial moral issues of our day,
whether it be abortion, euthanasia, fetal research, infertility
therapies, health care reform, or genetic therapy. Instead,
we seem to invest the process of giving information and
obtaining consent with far more absolute moral importance
than it deserves. We avoid divisiveness by steering clear of
any limitations on the freedom of "self-determining" indi-

viduals to choose, whether their free choices build up or tear down the common good.[161]

Such "free and informed" consent was a major ingredient and legacy of the Nuremberg trials. Yet if we avoid the substantive issues, we can produce a pluralism of practice with no other limit than consent. The value and importance of choice must be discussed, but so also must the worth of the goods chosen and their relative priorities, and whether other goods are being neglected or acted against in the process. Even within the confines of the death camps, Professor Schumann insisted on signed consents from the mothers of young Gypsy girls on whom he performed experimental sterilization procedures.[162] At other times, entire blocks of prisoners were locked up and deprived of all food and water for up to three days. Such procedures usually produced "volunteers." Review of Mengele's twin research and the other "Nazi research" shows that much of Nazi "medicine" was sadistic and pointless; reams of witnessed, fully informed consent could not make it moral. In today's society, for example, could the consent of some to be euthanized have undesirable effects on society in general? In short, consent does not make morality. Nor can the medical profession, or even an entire society, be trusted to run on moral autopilot.

Dan Maguire presents a critique of the Nazi analogy and finds little use for it in contemporary debates about euthanasia. He presents the Nazi analogy argument as follows: The grand scale German euthanasia program began on a small scale and involved only the severely and hopelessly sick. Once it began, however, it grew and spread to involve hundreds of thousands of "socially unproductive, defective, and eventually racially 'tainted' persons. 'Useless eaters' Hitler called them."[163] Since all this started from small beginnings, those who accept the Nazi analogy warn, if we allow any such similar small beginnings, we shall fall into Nazi excess.

Maguire urges caution in accepting the logic of this argument. He applies the same logic to argue that all killing, even self-defense, should be banned. All society should be absolute pacifists to preclude the "small beginning" of a war, which might once again turn into *Blitzkrieg*.

He points out several striking differences between our situation and Nazi Germany. First, Nazi euthanasia was not motivated by a concern for the individual. It was designed to save society's precious resources, which were not to be wasted on useless individuals. The motif of individual rights is not as deeply ingrained in the German society as it is in our own. Nor is our society so homogenous as German society. As Maguire puts it, "Our pluralism is incorrigible."[164] Third, our situation is different precisely because the Nazi experience has changed our individual and collective memories and our moral imaginations forever. Fourth, Maguire would argue that the question of voluntary dying is being examined in a climate that asks whether dying may be reevaluated as a possible good, not in the context of utilitarian values of certain lives over other lives. At least this is the ideal climate in which the moral argument should occur. Maguire's critics would argue that financial and utilitarian concerns really fuel the discussion, especially in the managed care climate of contemporary American medicine.

William F. May accepts the Nazi analogy and fears, not the slippery slope into Nazi genocide, but "marketplace seduction." May claims that we ought to fear the dictator who makes us do what we do not want to do less than the seducer who tempts us to do what we ought not do. We ought not fear a dictator who commands us to "Kill them!" as much as the "sweet talk of money. We've got better uses for that money than to make Grandpa's life bearable. Let him go and let's get on with it!" The Netherlands, with its generous health care coverage, has problems controlling euthanasia. It should be no problem to imagine what difficulties will multiply in the United States "with a population ravenously dedicated to its own quality of life."[165]

The Dutch Experience

The experience in the Netherlands illustrates several problems with the "merciful" administration of death. While euthanasia as such is technically illegal in the Netherlands, physicians who adhere to three important conditions recognized by the courts and endorsed by the State Commission on Euthanasia in 1985 are, in practice, not subject to criminal sanctions.

1. *Voluntariness.* The patient's request must be persistent, conscious, and freely made.
2. *Unbearable Suffering.* The patient's suffering, including but not limited to physical pain, cannot be relieved by any other means. Both the physician and the patient must consider that the patient is beyond recovery and that the condition cannot be ameliorated.
3. *Consultation.* The attending physician must consult with a colleague regarding the patient's condition and both the genuineness and appropriateness of the request for euthanasia.[166]

It is difficult for an American to arrive at a clear understanding of the status of euthanasia in Dutch society, since it is technically illegal (prohibited by Article 293 of the Dutch Penal Code), yet openly discussed and practiced.[167] It may be slightly analogous to the circumstances under which Dr. Jack Kevorkian has so far been able to successfully avoid conviction for his assisted suicides.[168] There is more official sanction of the practice in the

Netherlands, however, and no tension exists between state prosecutors and physicians acting in accord with the above three principles.

Those practices *not* considered euthanasia under Dutch law are the patient's refusal of life-sustaining treatment (either refusing to initiate it or insisting that it be withdrawn), abstinence from medically futile treatment, or administration of narcotic analgesics for pain relief, which may hasten death or impair consciousness.

Some of the difficulty in understanding the circumstances in the Netherlands may stem from the apparent confusion among Dutch physicians as to which cases of "euthanasia" they must report. Many physicians do not carefully maintain the distinction between euthanasia (the deliberate termination of life at the patient's request), and forgoing treatment. (As we will see, this may also include the *involuntary* termination of life.) The overall incidence of euthanasia was probably between four thousand and six thousand cases annually, between 3–4.5 percent of all deaths.

Those making the request for euthanasia were most commonly diagnosed with incurable malignancy (70%), chronic degenerative neurological disease (10%), or pulmonary disease (10%). The prominence given to intractable pain as a reason for requesting euthanasia may be misleading, for although poor pain control was still a leading reason for the request for euthanasia, intractable nausea or vomiting, incontinence, or the deterioration of other bodily functions become equally cogent reasons for insisting upon euthanasia.[169]

What has been the experience of this "legalized" or at least court-sanctioned euthanasia?

Several effects have been noted: (1) The difficulty in accurate reporting and statistics tabulation; perhaps understandable if euthanasia still technically remains a crime under Dutch law. (2) The tendency of physicians to admittedly administer euthanasia *involuntarily,* that is when not specifically requested by the patient. Sanctioned euthanasia in the case of an unresponsive patient's failure to die when life support is withdrawn is one example of how the definition and application of voluntary euthanasia may be extended to involuntary euthanasia.

Dan Callahan, among others, points out the contradiction between the self-determination argument and the tendency for some physicians to act on behalf of the patient's unspoken wishes by performing involuntary euthanasia. Having, on the one hand, established the all-important right to self-determination, one is prepared to hand it over to someone else by proxy, or in the case of the incompetent patient, to allow someone else to exercise this right on one's behalf.

Herbert Hendin, a New York psychiatrist, researched the Dutch experience by visiting the Netherlands and interviewing Dutch physicians and public policy planners. The more he heard and saw, the more shocked he became "not only at the number of what could only be called wrongful deaths but at the Dutch insistence on defending what seemed indefensible."[170] Hendin claims that the doctors who help set Dutch euthanasia policies are aware that euthanasia is "basically out of control in the Netherlands."[171]

Hendin does not bother discussing the theoretical niceties of the slippery slope argument. In his view, the Netherlands has already moved from assisted suicide to euthanasia, from euthanasia of the terminally ill to euthanasia for chronic physical illness to euthanasia for psychological distress (even insufficiently treated), and from voluntary euthanasia to involuntary euthanasia (which the Dutch physicians euphemistically call "termination of the patient without explicit request").

The Dutch government's own commissioned research, the Remmelink Report, has documented that in more than a thousand cases a year, doctors actively cause or hasten death without the patients' request.[172] Hendin documents in his book that virtually every guideline established by the Dutch to regulate euthanasia has been modified or violated with impunity. He cites examples: a grief-stricken social worker in clinical depression, mourning the recent death of her two sons, is assisted in her suicide; a newly diagnosed HIV-positive forty-year-old male without any symptoms is helped to die.[173]

Hendin relates the decision of the highest Dutch court acquitting a psychiatrist who had assisted the suicide of his patient, a physically healthy fifty-year-old woman who had lost her two sons and had recently divorced her husband. The court found that the patient was competent to make the decision freely, that she had "irremediable" suffering, and that her doctor was compelled by overpowering force (*force majeure*) to put the welfare of his patient above the law (which technically prohibits euthanasia) and assist her in suicide. Hendin particularly dislikes the term *force majeure,* because it seems to remove moral agency from the hands of the physician, who cannot help but kill the patient.[174]

Of the more than one thousand cases in which physicians admitted that they actively caused or hastened death without any request from the patient, refractory pain was cited as the reason in 30 percent of the cases. The remaining 70 percent were killed for reasons that varied from "low quality of life" to "all treatment was withdrawn, but the patient did not die."[175] The Commission did not find these cases troublesome because the suffering of these patients had become "unbearable," and they usually would have died soon anyhow. Of the physicians questioned, 27 percent indicated that they had terminated the lives of patients without a request from the patient do so; another 32 percent could conceive of doing so.[176] Hendin claims that thousands of both competent and incompetent patients are being put to death without their consent in the Netherlands. He details one case where the physician took it upon himself to end the life of a nun who had excruciat-

75

ing pain, but whose religious beliefs prevented her from asking for death herself.[177]

A Dutch medical journal reported the example of a wife who no longer wished to care for her ailing husband. She issued an ultimatum: euthanasia or admission to a nursing home. The man, afraid of being left to the mercy of strangers in an unfamiliar place, chose to be killed. The doctor, even though he was aware of the coercion, ended the man's life.[178]

As Hendin put it, the people he met in the Netherlands on both sides of the euthanasia question were bright and caring. Yet, in the name of humanitarian goals, bright and compassionate people were wrongly ending other people's lives.[179]

Not all motivation may be "well-intentioned," however. One prominent Dutch physician was asked if he would perform euthanasia on a patient who felt himself to be a nuisance to his relatives, who wanted him dead so they could enjoy his estate. The physician indicated that he would, "because that kind of influence—these children wanting their money now—is the same kind of power from the past that shaped us all."[180] If the Dutch "guidelines" can be interpreted in so cavalier a fashion, "little more need be said about their inherent vagueness and elasticity."[181]

The notion that some of the American doctors who are now breaking the law by assisting in suicides would suddenly follow guidelines, if they were to be established, is not borne out by the Dutch experience. Nor do the facts of the cases that have been published, which violate many voluntary safeguards.[182]

Margaret Battin suggests that examining medical practice in contemporary Germany may be more helpful than in the Netherlands. Citing data to show support of Americans for assisted suicide rather than euthanasia, she contrasts Americans with the Dutch, who favor euthanasia rather than assisted suicide. Even though legal toleration of assisted suicide in the Netherlands is also allowed, the rates of practice are very much different: 1.8 percent of deaths involve euthanasia, while only 0.3 percent involve assisted suicide. The Germans, however, allow assisted suicide, but not euthanasia, perhaps because euthanasia is a term associated with the Nazis. Here are two countries with very different experiences with assisted death. In most countries that have legalized neither, physician-assisted suicide and euthanasia seem to be considered different only by the agent who administers the fatal dose of medication. Yet Germany has legalized only assisted suicide, and the Dutch, who could have either, prefer euthanasia.[183] Battin urges continued study of these significant cultural differences and moral preferences to help understand the debate in America.

There are several modest conclusions that can be drawn from the slippery slope argument and from the experience with euthanasia in Germany and the Netherlands.

—The average physician can be convinced to perform immoral acts and even, as a part of a group, to justify them.
—There is a history of moving from small to big in Nazi Germany when exceptions to the sanctity of human life are made.
—There is a history of moving from voluntary to involuntary in the Netherlands with court-sanctioned euthanasia.

In a secular environment inimical to theological argumentation, the slippery slope argument still cautions against the legalization of exceptions to time-honored, culturally sanctioned rules like the prohibitions against euthanasia and suicide. The psychological/sociological slippery slope argument, along with the history of euthanasia in Nazi Germany and its contemporary practice in the Netherlands, convince many of a need to maintain absolute prohibitions against euthanasia and physician-assisted suicide.

Some critics of the slippery slope argument see it as a scare tactic, a means of maintaining the status quo. They feel that sufficient safeguards can be built into a legalized system of euthanasia or physician-assisted suicide to prevent the abuses about which the slippery-slopers warn. The advocates of the slippery slope argument, on the other hand, are less confident of our legislative and ethical prudence.

Chapter 8 ■
Medical Professionalism

OPPONENTS OF EUTHANASIA ARGUE THAT the very nature of the medical profession prohibits physicians not only from killing their patients, but even from cooperating in their suicides. A healer can neither deliberately hasten nor deliver death. Advocates of euthanasia deny this. They claim that the role of physician is sanctioned and regulated by society, not intrinsically determined by a professional code of ethics. They see the obligation of the physician both to cure the patient and to alleviate suffering. When cure is not possible, the physician must continue to help the patient by ending his or her suffering, even if it is necessary to take the sufferer's life to do so. Some ethicists even feel that if a fully competent, informed patient who is suffering unbearably seeks help from a physician to help end his or her own life, the physician is duty-bound to assist.

Advocates of euthanasia in the Netherlands have given physicians an important role in the administration of this societally sanctioned, but still technically illegal, procedure. Dan Brock contends that euthanasia does not violate the "moral center of medicine": respect for the patient's self-determination and promotion of the patient's well-being. It is not in the patients' well being, in his view, to "prolong their lives as such, without regard to whether those patients want their lives preserved, or judge their preservation a benefit to them."[184] When cure is not possible, the realistic physician willing to perform euthanasia on his or her patients honors the patient's self-determination and acts in the patient's best interests.

Others insist that medicine is an inherently ethical activity, in which technique and conduct are both ordered in relation to an overarching good, the naturally given end of health.[185] Besides the philosophical issues involved, there are practical social reasons why euthanasia goes counter to the medical profession. Euthanasia may divert money from adequate care for the dying. It will subvert the role of physician as healer and erode patient trust in their physician.[186]

In recent years, codes of professional ethics have changed in response to market forces, state and federal legislation, and patient demands. The profession is less paternalistic than it had been. There is far greater emphasis on the informed consent of the patient, who is accorded much greater voice in deciding diagnostic and therapeutic strategies. While many of these changes are good, there has also been a tendency to view the patient as a "consumer" and to provide services which keep the customer satisfied. Are fearful patients who demand euthanasia services from their physicians interfering with the very foundation of medical ethics?

The model one uses to image the nature of the healing art and science of medicine influences whether euthanasia can be accepted as an appropriate professional activity. The models of medical ethics cannot be discussed here in detail, but several models should be mentioned: (1) the engineering model, (2) the priestly model, (3) the collegial model, (4) the contractual model, and (5) the covenant model.[187]

In the priestly model, the physician's expertise in medical matters is considered to confer wisdom about life in general. The primary duty of the physician in this model is *primum non nocere,* above all do no harm. Physicians tend to assume the dominant decision-making role in this model, and can fail to adequately respect the patient's autonomy.[188]

In the collegial model, the physician and patient cooperate in pursuing a common goal, which may vary as widely as curing an illness at all costs, and simply providing palliative care. A relationship of mutual trust and ongoing dialogue is essential to this model.[189]

William F. May describes the characteristics of covenantal professional ethics of medicine. He discusses the requisite virtues for the medical profession—integrity, prudence, fidelity, courage, public-spiritedness, hope, and gratitude—as well as the essential elements of biblical covenant: gift, exchange of promises that shape all subsequent activity and are recalled in ritual. He criticizes those who would uproot the notions of covenant from its biblical soil.[190]

While the engineering model views the physician as a technically skilled medical salesperson whose expertise is for sale to any knowledgeable, well-informed consumer of medical services, the covenant model does not view the relationship between physician and patient as strictly business or financial, but instead engages biblical notions of steadfastness, fidelity, and nonmaleficence. The covenantal relationship is held to a higher standard of duty and mutual obligation. The engineering model would not necessarily have internal standards that would prohibit a physician from offering euthanasia services to willing patients, while a covenantal model probably would. Some speculate that grounding a professional ethic within a covenantal model might be the only way to incorporate spiritual values into the medical profession in a pluralistic society.

Even though contemporary philosophers since Kant and Heidegger have difficulty grounding metaphysics, and though many would have difficulty accepting the teleological view of the universe espoused by Aquinas, some medical ethicists have attempted to ground medical ethics in what they hold to be the intrinsically ordered healing relationship between physician and patient. The very nature of the healing relationship itself, they assert, would preclude physician-assisted suicide or euthanasia, even at the patient's request. Without attempting to elaborate an entire cosmology, they would hold that the relationship between healer and patient has its own internally directed goal, which cannot include harming the patient or hastening the patient's death. Still others talk of the virtues required by the practice of medicine. In their view the virtues (such as beneficence and fidelity) provide overarching guidance for the physician-patient relationship. Some others view the physician-patient relationship as a covenant.

Specific details about the nature of medical ethics may vary, but these theorists all agree that the relationship between physician and patient is not simply a business relationship. There is a code of ethics inherent in medicine, which holds the physician accountable to something other than the patient's wishes or demands.[191]

Two issues related to the euthanasia question are directly influenced by the view one has of the nature of the physician-patient relationship: the role of self-determination and the potential for conflict of interest in the current managed care system.

We have already seen that some believe patient autonomy to be so important that a physician has an obligation to honor the patient's request for assisted suicide or even active euthanasia. Some ethicists claim that the physician is able to offer such services to patients without necessarily adopting the patient's values. The engineering and contractual models of medical ethics would support such a position. Critics of these models point out, however, that the physician is also an autonomous individual, one who needs to rationalize his or her professional decisions with his or her own ethic. The physician cannot simply adopt the patient's ethics as sufficient reason for acting.

The physician's agreement to perform euthanasia or assisted suicide, then, involves a complex series of judgments about which lives are worth living. But the physician-healer is not entitled to make such judgments, especially since he or she operates from a superior position of power and authority. A covenantal model would not support harming a patient, even at the patient's own request. Furthermore, it would enjoin the physician to have a clearly articulated personal ethic of just exactly what kinds of professional behavior might be harmful to patients.

An engineering model of medical ethics might not be alarmed at the shifts of power occurring in the medical marketplace as a result of the emergence of for-profit Health Maintenance Organizations. In a *caveat emptor* medical environment, a patient may contract for euthanasia services as he or she sees fit. Physicians are not forced to offer such services, nor are patients forced to accept them. A covenant model, on the other hand, warns against allowing the doctor-patient relationship to be influenced by factors other than the patient's best interests. Cost containment measures have already become a prominent feature of managed care plans; economic incentives to practice euthanasia and to offer physician-assisted suicide could become enormous. A covenantal model of medical ethics might lead one to conclude that because of the dangers of abuse, euthanasia and physician-assisted suicide should not be offered in the present medical marketplace. Critics point to the major shortcomings in the distribution of medical care and fear that euthanasia and assisted suicide may only exacerbate such injustices.

The current debate over euthanasia and physician-assisted suicide has certainly challenged the medical profession to examine its ethical underpinnings. While many physicians feel that their

83

professional responsibility would never allow them to directly kill their patients or to hasten their deaths, others see no such moral prohibition. Continued discussion among physicians, health care planners, ethicists, and theologians will hopefully clarify the nature of the physician-patient relationship in our changing health care environment.

Chapter 9 ■
Conclusions and Commentary

IN MY OPINION, the evidence overwhelmingly supports the proposal that we maintain our stringent prohibitions against legalized euthanasia and physician-assisted suicide in America. All the while, we must redouble our efforts to render compassionate and freely available care to all Americans at all stages of their lives.

Legalizing euthanasia will have drastic implications for the physician-patient relationship. Patient trust of physicians has been strained by recent changes in the medical marketplace and the negative gatekeeping practices of certain HMOs. How much more will trust be eroded when the family physician is authorized under certain circumstances to kill you?[192] Fears that the availability of euthanasia may dramatically reduce the funds available for care near the end of life may be well founded. The economic and social pressures to end an otherwise costly terminal illness by euthanasia would be very great in our current health care system.

The tragic circumstances of some patients' deaths require specific solutions, not broad-based exemptions from the prohibitions against taking human life. Most patients with intractable pain can be helped with expert management of analgesia (understanding the principle of double effect and the possibility, even the likelihood, that effective pain management will shorten the individual's life). The individual in terrible psychic distress who faces terminal illness, or any other circumstance of life that he or she considers unbearable, deserves our care and compassion— not encouragement to put an end to suffering by ending his or her life!

The arguments against euthanasia are difficult to make in a pluralistic society. Without appeal to the teachings of Sacred Scripture or the tradition of Christian teachings and the consistently pro-life pronouncements of the magisterium, the absolute prohibition against euthanasia seems difficult to defend.

It becomes important then, to examine the arguments against euthanasia that are not specifically grounded in Christian claims. Here, I believe there is no single argument that can win the day, but rather a preponderance of evidence. Appeal can be made to the common good and the physician-patient relationship to ground arguments against euthanasia. The task is not easy, since both concepts are undermined by trends in contemporary American society.

The idea of a society's "common good" is as old as antiquity itself,[193] and has not been exclusively associated with a religious context. Nonetheless, in this age of PAC groups and political influence peddling, "common good" language is not our *lingua franca.* The strident debates over abortion, Social Security funding, health care, and welfare reform demonstrate how difficult it is for politicians and citizens alike to consider the common good. At the same time, authority of all kinds has been called into question. Enlightened reason no longer challenges only kings and priests, but political leaders and physicians, even scientific reason itself. Religious and civic leaders must nevertheless try to reawaken our sense of the common good. Professional societies and religious groups can gain respect by their integrity, leadership, and advocacy for the powerless.

William F. May has recently called for reawakening the virtue of "public-spiritedness," which he defines as the "art of acting in concert with others for the common good in the production, distribution, and quality control of health care."[194] He calls not only for commutative justice in the delivery of health care, but also distributive justice, including *pro bono publico* work.[195]

Even putting the theoretical form of the slippery slope argument aside, there is persuasive data that the psychological and "political" form of the argument may hold. While the Nazi analogy can sometimes be used as a scare tactic, the potential political and economic manipulation of euthanasia in a modern society must not be overlooked. Many already consider euthanasia in the Netherlands to be "out of control."[196] American jurisprudence has already extended the "right" to an abortion to women who are mentally disabled and incompetent—a ready-made judicial slippery slope from voluntary to involuntary euthanasia should mercy killing be legalized. How would the incompetent individual's "right" to euthanasia or physician-assisted suicide be exercised, and by whom?

The medical profession is in a unique position to exercise moral leadership in this debate. The public can be educated about their right to refuse burdensome medical care; the fear of being trapped on high-tech medical machinery can be lessened. Mechanisms to exercise this right of refusal must be more widely instituted and then respected. Physicians can become more expert in managing end-of-life care, including adequate analgesia; referrals can be made more liberally until such expertise is more widespread. Physicians can recapture the best traditions of medicine and refuse to become "hired syringes" for those seeking unacceptable solutions to human disease and suffering. Physicians, if they listen with understanding and patience, can extend a compassionate, helping hand to desperate patients asking for euthanasia, instead of a fatal intravenous bolus of morphine.

Finally, the medical profession can interact constructively with theologians and bishops in developing compassionate, coherent guidelines for the management of terminally ill and permanently unconscious patients, and pastoral guidelines for their families and caregivers. This will become even more important as medical advances in intensive care continue and the medical criteria for death evolve. We can anticipate that the definition of terminal illness will continue to change and that the measures available to forestall death will advance. The challenge to reach a consensus on the obligation to provide nutrition and hydration for the permanently unconscious person is only one of many that will arise in the months and years ahead. Theologians must dialogue with physicians not only on technical medical issues, but on the meaning of the physician-patient relationship and the nature of the human person as well.

Notes ■

1. Congregation for the Doctrine of the Faith, *Declaration on Euthanasia* (Rome: 1980), Section II.

2. Ron Hamel, ed., *Choosing Death: Active Euthanasia, Religion and the Public Debate* (Philadelphia: Trinity Press, 1991), 41. Some authors have used the term *passive euthanasia* to refer to the morally permissible refusal of excessively burdensome treatment; others reserve the use of this term for directly intended, and hence illicit, passive suicide.

3. Short-acting phenobarbiturates are well absorbed from the gastrointestinal tract and act synergistically with alcohol. Their effect can be guaranteed with a plastic bag over the head for suffocation. This is a "recipe" in many do-it-yourself suicide books, like Derek Humphry's *Final Exit* (Secaucus, N.J.: Carol Publishing, 1991).

4. Richard M. Gula, *Euthanasia: Moral and Pastoral Perspectives* (Mahwah, N.J.: Paulist Press, 1994), 6–7.

5. Source: Adapted from W. Bradford Patterson and Ezekiel J. Emanuel, eds. "Special Article: Ethics Rounds," *Journal of Clinical Oncology* 7 (July 1994): 1518, table 1.

6. Edwin R. DuBose, "A Brief Historical Perspective," in *Choosing Death,* ed. Ron Hamel (Philadephia: Trinity Press, 1991), 16.

7. Ezekiel J. Emanuel, "The History of Euthanasia Debates in the United States and Britain," *Annals of Internal Medicine* 121 (15 November 1994): 793.

8. DuBose, 16.

9. John J. Paris, "Notes on Moral Theology: Active Euthanasia," *Theological Studies* 53 (1992): 116.

10. DuBose, 18.

11. Ibid.

12. Emanuel, 793–95.

13. DuBose, 17.

14. Ibid., 18.

15. Socrates as quoted by DuBose, 18.

16. The Hippocratic oath as quoted by DuBose, 18. See also Paul Carrick, *Medical Ethics in Antiquity: Philosophical Perspectives on Abortion and Euthanasia* (Boston: D. Reidel Publishing, 1985), 96. Carrick states that the Hippocratic oath was probably framed by "some sort of reform group in Greek medical practice"

and probably constituted "a relatively small group of physicians." Carrick, even more than DuBose, cautions not to generalize conclusions about the acceptability of abortion in Greek and Roman society to arguments made today. Abortion and even infanticide were perfectly legal and widely practiced. Carrick discusses the position of each of the major classical philosophers on euthanasia and suicide. Aristotle's views are particularly important since both Augustine and Aquinas adapted them.

17. DuBose, 19.

18. Carrick, 158.

19. DuBose, 21.

20. Emanuel, 793.

21. Frances Bacon, *New Atlantis,* as quoted by Emanuel, 793, n. 18.

22. David Hume, *On Suicide,* as quoted by Emanuel, 794, n. 20.

23. Emanuel, 794.

24. "The Moral Side of Euthanasia." JAMA 1885 (5): 382–83 as quoted by Emanuel, 795, n. 38.

25. Emanuel, 795.

26. Ibid., 796.

27. On the significant academic debate on compulsory sterilization in America, see Robert J. Lifton, *The Nazi Doctors: Medical Killing and the Psychology of Genocide* (HarperCollins: New

York, 1986), chaps. 1 and 2. See also Foster Kennedy's article advocating the compulsory sterilization and/or euthanasia of the congenitally deformed, "The Problem of Social Control of the Congenitally Defective: Education, Sterilization, Euthanasia," *American Journal of Psychiatry* 99 (1942): 17–22.

28. Emanuel, 796. This article seems similar to the contemporary confession of the anonymous physician author of "It's All Over, Debbie." See note 36.

29. Paris, 116.

30. Abraham Wolbarst, "The Doctor Looks at Euthanasia" as quoted by Paris, 116.

31. Paris, 116.

32. Ibid., 113.

33. Fenella Rouse, "Practicing the PSDA," *Hastings Center Report Supplement* 21 (Sept./Oct. 1991): S2.

34. Elizabeth L. McCloskey, "The Spirit of the PSDA," *Hastings Center Report Supplement* 21 (Sept./Oct. 1991): S14.

35. See, for example, Derek Humphry, *Final Exit* (Secaucus, N.J.: Carol Publishing, 1991).

36. Anonymous, "It's All Over, Debbie," *The Journal of the American Medical Association* 259 (1988): 272. The article is also reprinted in Kenneth R. Overberg, ed., *Mercy or Murder: Euthanasia, Morality and Public Policy* (Kansas City: Sheed & Ward, 1993), 56–59.

37. Paris, 118. Willard Gayland, Leon R. Kass, Edmund D. Pellegrino, and Mark Siegler, "Doctors Must Not Kill," *The Journal of the American Medical Association* 259 (1988), 2139–40. Also in Overberg, *Mercy or Murder,* 125–29.

38. Sidney H. Wanzer, M.D., Daniel D. Federman, M.D., et. al. "The Physician's Responsibility toward Hopelessly Ill Patients: A Second Look," *New England Journal of Medicine* 320, no. 13 (March 30, 1989): 844–49. Also reprinted in Overberg, 38–53.

39. Overberg, 51.

40. Ibid., 53.

41. Emanuel, 797.

42. Ibid., 800.

43. Kevin O'Rourke, "Value Conflicts Raised by Physician-Assisted Suicide," *Linacre Quarterly* 57 (August 1990): 42. Augustine, however, was influential in developing the just war theory, and so the prohibition against killing was seen as subordinate to the right of those in authority to wage war.

44. Ibid.

45. Ibid.

46. DuBose, 21.

47. Perhaps Paolo Zacchia, a Roman physician (1621) and the moral manuals of St. Alphonsus Liguori (1789) should also receive mention. Liguori was declared a saint (1839), a doctor of the church (1871), and the patron of moral theology (1950).

48. Kevin W. Wildes, "Ordinary and Extraordinary Means and the Quality of Life," *Theological Studies* 57 (1996): 501–2.

49. Wildes, 506. Archbishop Cronin's thesis is reprinted in *Conserving Human Life,* ed. Russell E. Smith (Braintree, Mass.: Pope John Center, 1989), 1–145.

50. Pope Pius XII, *Mystici Corporis,* Acta Apostolica Sedis, 35 (July 20, 1943), 239, as quoted by O'Rourke, "Value Conflicts," 43–44, n. 10. See above. It is interesting to note the similarity between this and John Paul II's writings. An appeal is made to natural law, biblical grounding, and emphasis on the universal common good. In fact, John Paul II uses the Cain and Abel story of Gn 4 in *Evangelium vitae.*

51. O'Rourke, "Value Conflicts," 44. *Casti connubii* condemned compulsory sterilization performed for eugenic reasons. The fact that a few German Catholic theologians were trying to rationalize Nazi eugenics with Catholic morality is scandalous and interesting, but since they were not also physicians, beside the point.

52. *Gaudium et spes,* 27.

53. Emanuel, "The History of Euthanasia Debates," 797.

54. *Declaration on Euthanasia,* section II.

55. O'Rourke, "Value Conflicts," 44.

56. John Paul II, *Evangelium vitae,* 65. The discussion of the document presented here also references paragraphs 66 (euthanasia in the Netherlands), 73 (conscientious objection), 81 (defense of human dignity), 89 (health care as an affirmation of life).

57. *Salvifici doloris,* 19.

58. Ibid., 27.

59. Ibid.

60. William F. May, *Active Euthanasia and Health Care Reform: Testing the Medical Covenant* (Grand Rapids: William B. Eerdmans, 1996), 18.

61. A recent survey of physicians in Washington State disclosed that 54 percent of the physicians surveyed felt that euthanasia should be legalized in some situations, with 33 percent willing to perform it; 53 percent thought that physician-assisted suicide should be legalized in some situations, and 40 percent reported willingness to assist in it. J. S. Cohen et al., "Attitudes Toward Physician-Assisted Suicide and Euthanasia Among Physicians in Washington State," *New England Journal of Medicine* 331 (14 July 1994): 89–94.

When asked to choose between legalization of physician-assisted suicide or an explicit ban, 56 percent of physicians and 66 percent of the public support its legalization. If physician-assisted suicide were legal, 35 percent of physicians said they might participate if requested; 22 percent would participate in either assisted suicide or voluntary euthanasia; and 13 percent would participate only in assisted suicide. J. G. Bachman et al., "Attitudes of Michigan Physicians and the Public Toward Legalizing Physician-Assisted Suicide and Voluntary Euthanasia," *New England Journal of Medicine* 334 (1 Feb. 1996): 303–9.

62. Gula, *Euthanasia,* 10.

63. Ibid.

64. Ibid.

65. Daniel Callahan, *The Troubled Dream of Life* (New York: Simon and Schuster, 1993), 11.

66. Dan Brock, "Voluntary Active Euthanasia," *Hastings Center Report* 22 (March/April 1992): 11.

67. *Autonomy* is more often called *self-determination* in papal documents. Cf. *Evangelium vitae,* 54–56.

68. *Veritatis splendor,* 55–59.

69. *Evangelium vitae,* 65.

70. Ibid., 71.

71. M. Cathleen Kaveny, "Assisted Suicide, Euthanasia and the Law," *Theological Studies* 58 (1997): 124–48.

72. Brock, 11.

73. Herbert Hendin, *Seduced by Death: Doctors, Patients and the Dutch Cure* (New York: W. W. Norton & Company, 1997), 110.

74. Dan Callahan, "When Self-Determination Runs Amok," *Hastings Center Report* 22 (March/April 1992): 52–55.

75. Hendin, 30–32.

76. Kaveny, 125.

77. William F. May, 26.

78. See, for example, S. D. Block and J. A. Billings, "Patient Requests to Hasten Death: Evaluation and Management in Terminal Care," *Archives of Internal Medicine* 154 (Sept. 1994): 2039–47; H. M. Cochinov and K. G. Wilson, "The Euthanasia Debate: Attitudes, Practices and Psychiatric Considerations," *Canadian Journal of Psychiatry* 40 (Dec. 1995): 593–602; Ezekiel J. Emanuel, "Euthanasia and Physician-Assisted Suicide: Attitudes and Experiences of Oncology Patients, Oncologists and the Public," *Lancet* 347 (29 June 1996): 1805–10; M. M. Burgess, "The Medicalization of Dying," *Journal of Medical Philosophy* 18 (June 1993): 269–79; D. F. Kelly, "Alternative to Physician-Assisted Suicide," *American Journal of Otolaryngology* 16 (May/June 1995): 181–85.

79. Hendin, 115–16.

80. Ibid., 119.

81. Ibid., 120.

82. William F. May, 28.

83. Ibid., 16.

84. Ibid., 36.

85. Ibid.

86. *Report of the Dutch Governmental Committee on Euthanasia,* 343, as quoted by William F. May, 39.

87. William F. May, 39.

88. Leon Kass, in a foreword to Carlos Gomez, *Regulating*

Death: Euthanasia and the Case of the Netherlands (New York: Free Press, 1991) p. x, as quoted by William F. May, 40, n. 32.

89. Carlos Gomez, *Regulating Death,* 134, as quoted by William F. May, 40, n. 33.

90. Gula, *Euthanasia,* 14.

91. Ibid.

92. Brock, 14.

93. Ibid.

94. Callahan, 52. Euthanasia goes against the common good. We will examine this claim in more detail in chapter 6.

95. Charles E. Curran, "Cooperation: Toward a Revision of the Concept and Its Application," *Linacre Quarterly* 41 (August 1974): 154.

96. James F. Keenan, "Prophylactics, Toleration and Cooperation: Contemporary Problems and Traditional Principles," *International Philosophical Quarterly* XXIX (June 1989): 205–220. See also Judith Lee Kissell, "Cooperation with Evil: Its Contemporary Relevance," *Linacre Quarterly* 62 (February 1995): 33–45.

97. Richard M. Gula, *Reason Informed by Faith: Foundations of Catholic Morality* (New York/Mahwah, NJ: Paulist Press), 1989, p. 265–70.

98. National Conference of Catholic Bishops, *Ethical and Religious Directives for Catholic Health-Care Services*

(Washington, D.C.: United States Catholic Conference, 1995): Part VI and Appendix.

99. It should be noted here that this argument, in one form or other, extends all the way back to antiquity. Emanuel contends that it has little or nothing to do with modern life-sustaining therapy. J. F. Tuohey asserts that a society must not act *only* out of compassion or mercy, but with reason as well. A reasoned approach to the plight of the dying will suggest other remedies than euthanasia, such as compassionate presence, adequate analgesia, etc. See J. F. Tuohey, "Mercy: An Insufficient Motive for Euthanasia," *Health Progress* 74 (Oct. 1993): 51–53.

100. William F. May, 28.

101. Ibid., 28.

102. Ibid., 29.

103. Ibid.

104. Ibid., 32.

105. *Ethical and Religious Directives,* Part V.

106. William F. May, 33.

107. Ibid., 34.

108. James Rachels, "Active and Passive Euthanasia," *New England Journal of Medicine* 292 (1975): 78–80.

109. Brock, 12.

110. Ibid., 13-14.

111. Ibid.

112. Ibid., 13.

113. William F. May, 16.

114. Ibid., 16-18.

115. Daniel C. Maguire, *Death by Choice,* 2d ed. (Garden City: Doubleday, 1984), 97.

116. Ibid., 98.

117. Surveys indicate that more physicians would be willing to participate in physician-assisted suicide than in euthanasia. See note 61.

118. This "clinical morality" has not been sufficiently explored by theoretical ethicists or moral theologians. More attention should perhaps be paid to the phenomenological analysis of the distinctions.

119. Maguire, 101.

120. Gula, *Reason Informed by Faith,* 270–72.

121. *Declaration on Euthanasia,* Section IV.

122. Ibid., Section II.

123. Bishop James T. McHugh, "Artificially Assisted Nutrition/ Hydration," *The Priest* (Jan. 1990): 32–34; William E. May et al.,

"Feeding and Hydrating the Permanently Unconscious and Other Vulnerable Persons," *Issues in Law and Medicine* 3 (Winter 1987): 203–11; William E. May, "Nutrition and Hydration: Moral Considerations: A Statement of the Catholic Bishops of Pennsylvania," *Linacre Quarterly* (Feb. 1992): 34–36.

124. Joseph Cardinal Bernardin, "Euthanasia: Ethical and Legal Challenge," (1988 address at University of Chicago Center for Clinical Medical Ethics) quoted in *The Churches Speak On: Euthanasia*, J. Gordon Melton, ed. (Detroit: Gale Research Inc., 1991), 30.

125. *Ethical and Religious Directives*, Directive 58.

126. Ibid., Part V, Introduction.

127. James F. Bresnahan, "Killing vs. Letting Die: A Moral Distinction Before the Courts," *America* 176 (1 Feb. 1997): 8–16.

128. Gula, *Euthanasia*, 15.

129. Ibid., 17.

130. See Robert Bellah et al., *Habits of the Heart* (New York and San Francisco: Harper and Row, 1986) for a critique of this state of contemporary American culture.

131. Hume, Cardinal Basil. "The Hinterland of Freedom: Morality and Solidarity." *The Month* (March 1994): 88–89. Cardinal Hume discusses the abstract virtue of solidarity in a very pastoral way. Pope John Paul II's *Sollicitudo rei socialis* discusses the virture of solidarity as well.

132. John Hardwig, "Is There a Duty to Die?" *Hastings Center Report* 27 (1997): 34–42.

133. Pope John Paul II's defense of absolute moral norms in both *Veritatis splendor* and *Evangelium vitae* militates against even setting foot upon the slippery slope.

134. This book will not discuss the relevance of legalized abortion and its judicial and legislative aftermath to the euthanasia question. Many believe, however, that its emphasis on the "right to choose" created the climate in which enthusiasm for euthanasia seems to be growing. I believe this argument has validity, but its discussion is beyond the scope of this work.

In addition, there may be an American judicial "slippery slope." See Kaveny article.

135. Tom L. Beauchamp and James F. Childress, *Principles of Biomedical Ethics,* 3d ed. (New York: Oxford University Press, 1989), 141.

136. Gerald Dworkin, "Dangerous Ground?" review of *Down the Slippery Slope: Arguing in Applied Ethics,* by David Lamb, *Hastings Center Report* 20 (May/June 1990): 42.

137. David Lamb, *Down the Slippery Slope: Arguing the Applied Ethics,* 7, as quoted by Dworkin, 42. It would seem the argument moves from ontological to relative categories.

138. Lamb, 42, as quoted by Dworkin, 42. This logic drives a significant part of the New Jersey Bishops' statement on the necessity for providing food and hydration for the permanently unconscious patient.

139. Dworkin, 42.

140. Ibid., 42–43.

141. Beauchamp and Childress, 141.

142. Ibid., 140.

143. Brock, 20–21.

144. Beauchamp and Childress, 141.

145. John J. Michalczyk, ed., *Medicine, Ethics and the Third Reich: Historical and Contemporary Issues* (Kansas City: Sheed & Ward, 1994), 7.

146. Arthur Caplan, "The Relevance of the Holocaust to Current Bio-Medical Issues," in *Medicine, Ethics and the Third Reich*, 11–12.

147. Determining just what kind of care is mandatory for the permanently unconscious patient has gradually come before American courts. Can physicians and families either refuse to initiate certain life-sustaining therapies or interrupt once they have begun? The family of Karen Quinlan won the right to remove her from a respirator in 1976 after a prolonged court battle. She did not die, however, and survived ten more years in a persistent vegetative state. In 1990, the family of Nancy Cruzan won a similar court battle to permit cessation of tube feedings.

148. Robert N. Proctor, "Racial Hygiene: The Collaboration of Medicine and Nazism," in *Medicine, Ethics and the Third Reich*, 36.

149. Lifton, 24–25.

150. Ibid.

151. Proctor, 37.

152. Lifton, 65.

153. Ibid., 63.

154. Ibid., 65.

155. Ibid., 71.

156. Ibid., 76.

157. Ibid., 65–79.

158. Ibid., 93–94.

159. Proctor, 39.

160. Lifton and Michalczyk, for example.

161. Lisa Sowle Cahill, "Lessons We Have Learned?" in *Medicine, Ethics and the Third Reich,* 214.

162. Michalczyk, 137.

163. Maguire, 111.

164. Ibid., 112.

165. William F. May, 41.

166. Maurice A. M. deWachter, "Euthansia in the Netherlands." *Hastings Center Report* 22 (March/April): 23.

167. Ibid., 23–25.

168. Herbert Hendin provides fascinating biographical data on Kevorkian. He was first called "Dr. Death" during his medical residency in 1956 because of his interest in photographing the retinal vessels of patients at the moment of their death in the hope of devising some method to distinguish between coma, shock, and fainting. Later he published papers suggesting that medical experimentation be done on anesthetized death-row inmates lasting hours or even months, after which they would be given lethal doses of anesthetics. He noted that experiments on living humans would save the lives of innocent lab animals killed in the name of science.

He first coined the term "obitiatry" in connection with these experiments, later expanding it to mean a board-certified medical specialty that would train its practitioners in "medicide." He would divide the state of Michigan into eleven geographic zones, each with its own obitiatry headquarters and death clinic. He has published a paper describing the mechanics of how one would seek death within this newly created medical bureaucracy. See Hendin, 30–32.

169. Henk A. M. J. ten Have and Jos V. M. Weilie. "Euthanasia: Normal Medicial Practice?" *Hastings Center Report* 22 (March-April 1992): 34–35.

170. Hendin, 13.

171. "The doctors who help set Dutch euthanasia policies are aware that euthanasia is basically out of control in the Netherlands. They admitted this to me privately. Yet in their pub-

lic statements and articles they maintain that there are no serious problems. They not only attempt to suppress dissent from domestic critics, but actively work to promote and normalize euthanasia. Ibid., 14–15.

172. Ibid., 23.

173. Ibid., 131–34.

174. Ibid., 109–10.

175. Ibid., 76.

176. Ibid.

177. Ibid., 79.

178. Ibid., 93.

179. Ibid., 95.

180. Ibid., 108.

181. Ibid., 176.

182. Ibid., 178.

183. Margaret P. Battin, "Assisted Suicide: Lessons from Germany," *Hastings Center Report* 22 (March/April 1992): 44.

184. Brock, 16.

185. Leon R. Kass, "Neither for Love nor Money: Why Doctors Must Not Kill," in *Mercy or Murder: Euthanasia, Morality &*

Public Policy, ed. Kenneth R. Overberg, 113–15. Here are certainly echoes of Aristotle and Aquinas.

186. The refusal of the medical profession to become involved in capital punishment is pertinent here. Peter A. Singer and Mark Siegler, "Euthanasia: A Critique," in *Mercy or Murder,* ed. Overberg, 136.

187. Robert Veatch, "Models for Ethical Practice in a Revolutionary Age," *Hastings Center Report* (June 1972): 5–7.

188. Thomas M. Garrett, Harold W. Baillie, and Rosellen M. Garrett, *Health Care Ethics: Principle and Problems* (Englewood Cliffs: Prentice Hall, 1993), 19.

189. Ibid., 18.

190. William F. May, 63–83. He summarizes the contractual vs. covenantal models on pp. 6–9.

191. For a discussion of several of the models for medical ethics see my discussion in "The Ethical Physician as Negative Gatekeeper?" *Linacre Quarterly* 62 (August 1995): 15–25.

192. Based on the experience in the Netherlands, not fancifully imagined.

193. DuBose, 17–18.

194. William F. May, 75.

195. Ibid., 77.

196. Hendin, 14–15.

Bibliography ■

Angell, Marcia. "Euthanasia." *The New England Journal of Medicine* 319 (1988): 1348–50.

_____. "Prisoners of Technology: The Case of Nancy Cruzan." *The New England Journal of Medicine* 322 (1990): 1226–28.

_____. "The Case of Helga Wanglie: A New Kind of 'Right to Die' Case." *The New England Journal of Medicine* 325 (1991): 511–12.

Battin, Margaret P. "Assisted Suicide: Lessons from Germany." *Hastings Center Report* 22 (March/April 1992): 44–51.

Beauchamp, Tom L. and James F. Childress. *Principles of Biomedical Ethics,* 3d ed. New York: Oxford University Press, 1989.

Bernardin, Joseph Cardinal. "Euthanasia: Ethical and Legal Challenge." *Origins* (June 9 1988): 52–57.

_____. "Renewing the Covenant With Patients and Society." *Linacre Quarterly* 63 (February 1996): 3–9.

Block, S. D. and J. A. Billings. "Patient Requests to Hasten Death." *Archives of Internal Medicine* 154 (26 September 1994): 2039–47.

Branson, Roy. "The Physician-Patient Relation: Virtues, Obligations, and the Prophetic Vision." *Kennedy Institute of Ethics Journal* 6 (1996): 361–66.

Bresnahan, James F. "Killing vs. Letting Die: A Moral Distinction Before the Courts." *America* 176 (February 1, 1997): 8–16.

Brock, Dan. "Voluntary Active Euthanasia." *Hastings Center Report* 22 (March/April 1992): 10–22.

Burgess, John P. "Can I Know That My Time Has Come?: Euthanasia and Assisted Suicide." *Theology Today* 51 (July 1994): 204–218.

Cahill, Lisa Sowle. "Euthanasia: Continuing the Conversion." *Linacre Quarterly* 48 (August 1981): 243–45.

Callahan, Daniel. *The Troubled Dream of Life.* New York: Simon and Schuster, 1993.

_____. "When Self-Determination Runs Amok." *Hastings Center Report* 22 (March/April 1992): 52–55.

_____. "The Sanctity of Life Seduced: A Symposium on Medical Ethics." *First Things* 42 (April 1994): 13–27.

Campbell, Courtney S. "Religious Ethics and Active Euthanasia in a Pluralistic Society." *Kennedy Institute of Ethics Journal* 2 (September 1992): 253–77.

_____. "Religion and the Moral Meaning of Euthanasia." *Linacre Quarterly* 59 (November 1992): 15–28.

Campbell, Courtney S., Jan Hare, and Pam Matthews. "Conflicts of Conscience: Hospice and Assisted Suicide." *Hastings Center Report* 25 (May/June 1995): 36–43.

Capron, Alexander Morgan. "Euthanasia in the Netherlands: American Observations." *Hastings Center Report* 22 (March/April 1992): 30–33.

Carrick, Paul. *Medical Ethics in Antiquity: Philosophical Perspectives on Abortion and Euthanasia.* Boston: D. Reidel Publishing Company, 1985.

Cassel, C. K. "Morals and Moralism in the Debate Over Euthanasia and Assisted Suicide." *New England Journal of Medicine* 324 (16 May 1991): 1434–37.

Cassell, E. J. "The Nature of Suffering and the Goals of Medicine." *The New England Journal of Medicine* 306 (1982): 639–45.

Coleman, Gerald D. "Natural Law and the 'Declaration on Euthanasia.'" *Linacre Quarterly* 48 (August 1981): 259–64.

Congregation for the Doctrine of the Faith. *Declaration on Euthanasia.* Rome, 1980.

Crigger, Bette Jane, ed. "Practicing the PSDA." *Hastings Center Report* 21 (September/October 1990): S2–S16.

_____. "Dying Well: A Colloquy on Euthanasia and Assisted Suicide." *Hastings Center Report* 22 (March/April 1992): 6–55.

Curran, Charles E. "Cooperation: Toward a Revision of the Concept and Its Application." *Linacre Quarterly* 41 (August 1974): 152–67.

_____. *History and Contemporary Issues: Studies in Moral Theology.* New York: Continuum Publishing Company, 1996.

Doerflinger, Richard M. "Assisted Suicide: The Moral Equation." *Linacre Quarterly* 60 (November 1993): 22–28.

Dworkin, Gerald. "Dangerous Ground?" Review of *Down the Slippery Slope: Arguing in Applied Ethics* by David Lamb, in *Hastings Center Report* 20 (May/June 1990): 42–43.

Emanuel, Ezekiel J. "Euthanasia: Historical, Ethical and Empiric Perspectives." *Archives of Internal Medicine* 154 (1994): 1890–1901.

_____. "The History of Euthanasia Debates in the United States and Britain." *Annals of Internal Medicine* 121 (15 November 1994): 793–802.

_____. "Pain and Symptom Control." *Hematology Oncology Clinics of North America* 10 (February 1996): 41–56.

Engelhardt, H. Tristram. "Suffering, Meaning, and Bioethics." *Christian Bioethics* 2 (1996): 129–53.

Fisher, Anthony. "On Not Starving the Unconscious." *New Blackfriars* 74 (March 1993): 130–45.

Fleming, John I. "Euthanasia: Human Rights and Inalienability." *Linacre Quarterly* 63 (February 1966): 44–56.

Garver, Kenneth L. "Eugenics, Euthanasia and Genocide." *Linacre Quarterly* 59 (August 1992): 24–51.

Geis, Sally B. and Donald E. Messer, eds. *How Shall We Die?: Helping Christians Debate Assisted Suicide.* Nashville: Abindgon Press, 1997.

Gormally, Luke. "Euthanasia: Some Points in a Philosophical Polemic." *Linacre Quarterly* 57 (May 1990): 14–25.

Groarke, Louis. "Epicurus and Euthanasia." *Linacre Quarterly* 61 (May 1994): 91–94.

Grant, Edward R. "What in the World Is Going On? A Consideration of the California Euthanasia Proposal." *Linacre Quarterly* 57 (February 1990): 58–63.

Griesa, Thomas. "Assisted-Suicide Ban Ruled Constitutional." *Origins* 24 (January 23 1995): 497–503.

Gula, Richard M. *Euthanasia: Moral and Pastoral Perspectives.* New York/Mahwah, N.J.: Paulist Press, 1994.

Guroian, Vigen. *Life's Living Toward Dying.* Grand Rapids: William Eerdmans Publishing Company, 1996.

Hamel, Ron, ed. *Choosing Death: Active Euthanasia, Religion and the Public Debate.* Philadelphia: Trinity Press, 1991.

Hardwig, John. "Is There a Duty to Die?" *Hastings Center Report* 27 (March/April 1997): 34–42.

Hauerwas, Stanley. "Practicing Patience: How Christians Should Be Sick." *Christian Bioethics* 2 (1996): 202–21.

Have, Henk A. M. J. ten and Jos. V. M. Welie. "Euthanasia: Normal Medical Practice?" *Hastings Center Report* 22 (March/April 1992): 34–38.

Hendin, Herbert. *Seduced by Death: Doctors, Patients and the Dutch Cure.* New York: W. W. Norton & Company, 1997.

_____. "Selling Death and Dignity." *Hastings Center Report* 25 (May/June 1995): 18–23.

Holst, Lawrence E. "Do We Need More Help in Managing Our Death? A Look at Physician-Assisted Suicide." *The Journal of Pastoral Care* 47 (Winter 1993): 336–47.

Horan, Dennis J. and David Mall. *Death, Dying and Euthanasia.* Frederick, Maryland: Aletheai Books, 1980.

Howell, Joseph H. and William Frederick Sale, eds. *Life Choices: A Hastings Center Introduction to Bioethics.* Washington, D.C.: Georgetown University Press, 1995.

Humber, James M., Robert F. Almeder, and Gregg A. Kasting, eds. *Physician-Assisted Death.* Totowa, New Jersey: Humana Press, 1994.

Hume, Cardinal Basil. "The Hinterland of Freedom: Morality and Solidarity." *The Month* (March 1994): 88–92.

John Paul II. "(*Salvifici doloris*) On the Christian Meaning of Human Suffering," February 1984.

_____. "(*Evangelium vitae*) The Gospel of Life," March 25, 1995.

Kamisar, Y. "Are Laws Against Assisted Suicide Unconstitutional?" *Hastings Center Report* 23 (May/June 1993): 32–41.

_____. "The Ever Expanding Right to Die." *The Human Life Review* (Summer 1996): 33–36.

Kass, Leon R. "Suicide Made Easy." *Commentary* 92 (December 1991): 19–24.

Kass, Leon R. and Nelson Lund. "Courting Death: Assisted Suicide, Doctors and the Law." *Commentary* (December 1966): 17–29.

Kaveny, M. Cathleen. "Assisted Suicide, Euthanasia and the Law." *Theological Studies* 58 (March 1997): 124–48.

Keating, James and John Corbett. "Euthanasia and the Gift of Life." *Linacre Quarterly* (August 1996): 33–41.

Keenan, James F. "Prophylactics, Toleration and Cooperation: Contemporary Problems and Traditional Principles." *International Philosophical Quarterly* XXIX (June 1989): 205–20.

Keenan, James F. and Thomas R. Kopfensteiner. "The Principle

114

of Cooperation: Theologians Explain Material and Formal Cooperation." *Health Progress* 76 (April 1995): 23–27.

Keown, John. "On Regulating Death." *Hastings Center Report* 22 (March/April 1992): 39–43.

Kissell, Judith Lee. "Cooperation with Evil: Its Contemporary Relevance." *Linacre Quarterly* 62 (February 1995): 33–45.

Kohn, Marvin, ed. *Beneficient Euthanasia.* Buffalo, New York: Prometheus Books, 1975.

Lamb, David. *Down the Slippery Slope: Arguing in Applied Ethics.* New York: Routledge Chapman & Hall, 1988.

Lamb, Michael G. "A Thousand Lost Golfballs." *Linacre Quarterly* 55 (May 1988): 31–34.

Levada, William J., Archbishop. "Oregon's Vote on Measure 16." *Origins* 24 (December 1 1994): 431–32.

Lifton, Robert Jay. *The Nazi Doctors: Medical Killing and the Psychology of Genocide.* New York: HarperCollins, 1986.

Maguire, Daniel C. "Death by Choice: A Rejoinder." *Linacre Quarterly* 41 (May 1974): 141–43.

_____. *Death by Choice.* Second edition. Garden City: Doubleday & Company, 1984.

Mahony, Robert M., Cardinal. "Two statements on the Bouvia Case." *Linacre Quarterly* 55 (February 1988): 83–88.

Manning, Michael. "The Ethical Physician as Negative Gatekeeper?" *Linacre Quarterly* 62 (August 1995): 15–25.

Marx, Paul. "Euthanasia Worldwide." *Linacre Quarterly* 57 (August 1990): 27–49.

May, William E. Review of *Death by Choice,* by Daniel C. Maguire. *Linacre Quarterly* 41 (May 1974): 135–40.

_____. "Is There a Right to Die?" *Linacre Quarterly* 60 (November 1993): 34–44.

May, William F. *Active Euthanasia and Health Care Reform: Testing the Medical Covenant.* Grand Rapids: William B. Eerdmans Publishing Company, 1996.

McCormick, Richard A. and Robert Veatch. "The Preservation of Life and Self-Determination." *Theological Studies* 41 (June 1980): 390–96.

Melton, J. Gordon. *The Churches Speak on: Euthanasia.* Detroit: Gale Research, 1991.

Meserve, Harry C. "And Peace at the Last." *Journal of Religion and Health* 32 (Fall 1993): 157–62.

Michalczyk, John J., ed. *Medicine, Ethics and the Third Reich: Historical and Contemporary Issues.* Kansas City: Sheed & Ward, 1994.

Michigan Catholic Conference. "Physician-Assisted Suicide and Euthanasia." *Origins* 23 (June 17 1993): 63–64.

Miles, John. "Protecting Patient Self-Determination." *Health Progress* 72 (April 1991): 26–30.

Miles, Steven H. "Physician-Assisted Suicide and the Profession's Gyrocompass." *Hastings Center Report* 25 (May/June 1995): 17–18.

Miller, Franklin G. and Howard Brody. "Professional Integrity and Physician-Assisted Death." *Hastings Center Report* 25 (May/June 1995): 8–16.

Murchison, William. "Doctor Death, the Celebrity." *The Human Life Review* (Fall 1996): 7–14.

National Conference of Catholic Bishops. *Ethical and Religious Directives for Catholic Health Care Services.* Washington, D. C.: United States Catholic Conference, 1995.

Neuhaus, Richard John. "Never Again?" *First Things* 45 (August/September 1994): 66–68.

_____. "To Step Gingerly Over the Cliff." *First Things* 46 (October 1994): 78–82.

New York State Task Force on Life and the Law. "When Death Is Sought: Assisted Suicide and Euthanasia in the Medical Context." Chapter 6: Crafting Public Policy on Assisted Suicide and Euthanasia. May 1994: 117–48.

Norris, Patrick. "The Movement Toward Physician-Assisted Suicide: A Step in the Wrong Direction." *Linacre Quarterly* 63 (May 1996): 31–40.

Nuechterlein, James, ed. "The Sanctity of Life Seduced: A Symposium on Medical Ethics." *First Things* 42 (April 1994): 13–27.

O'Rourke, Kevin David. "Value Conflicts Raised by Physician-Assisted Suicide." *Linacre Quarterly* 57 (August 1990): 38–49.

O'Rourke, Kevin David and Philip Boyle. *Medical Ethics: Sources of Catholic Teachings.* St. Louis, Mo.: The Catholic Health Association of the United States, 1989.

Overberg, Kenneth R., ed. *Mercy or Murder: Euthanasia, Morality and Public Policy.* Kansas City: Sheed & Ward, 1993.

Paris, John J. "Notes on Moral Theology: Active Euthanasia." *Theological Studies* 53 (1992): 113–26.

Paterson, W. Bradford and Ezekiel J. Emanuel, eds. "Special Article: Ethics Rounds." *Journal of Clinical Oncology* 7 (July 1994): 1516–21.

Pellegrino, Edmund D., John P. Langan and John Collins Harvey, eds. *Catholic Perspectives on Medical Morals: Foundational Issues.* Boston: Kluwer Academic Publishers, 1989.

Pijnenborg, Loes, Paul J. Van der Maas, Johannes J. M. van Delden, and Caspar W. N. Looman. "Life-Terminating Acts Without Explicit Request of Patient." *Lancet* 341 (May 8, 1993): 1196–99.

Rachels, James, "Active and Passive Euthanasia," *New England Journal of Medicine* 292 (1975): 78–80.

Rae, Scott B. "The California Euthanasia Initiative." *Linacre Quarterly* 59 (November 1992): 5–14.

Ramsey, Paul. *Ethics at the Edges of Life: Medical and Legal Intersections.* New Haven: Yale University Press, 1978.

_____. *The Patient as Person.* New Haven: Yale University Press, 1970.

Schlogel, Herbert. "Euthanasia and Theology." *Theology Digest* 41 (Spring 1994): 15–19.

SSM Health Care System. "Ethical Issues and Legalizing Physician-Assisted Suicide." *Issues* 11 (September/October 1996): 1–8.

Tuohey, John F. "Euthanasia and Assisted Suicide: Is Mercy Sufficient?" *Linacre Quarterly* 60 (November 1993): 45–49.

Uhlmann, Michael M. "The Legal Logic of Euthanasia." *The Human Life Review* (Summer 1996): 23–31.

United States Catholic Conference. "A Framework for Comprehensive Health Care Reform." Washington, D.C.: United States Catholic Conference, 1993.

deWachter, Maurice A. M. "Euthanasia in the Netherlands." *Hastings Center Report* 22 (March/April 1992): 23–29.

Walter, James J. and Thomas A. Shannon, eds. *Quality of Life: The New Medical Dilemma.* New York/Mahwah, N.J.: Paulist Press, 1990.

Wanzer, S. H., D. D. Federman, S. J. Adelstein, et al. "The

Physician's Responsibility Toward Hopelessly Ill Patients: A Second Look." *New England Journal of Medicine* 320 (1989): 844–49.

Wildes, Kevin W. "Ordinary and Extraordinary Means and the Quality of Life." *Theological Studies* 57 (1996): 500–12.

Wildes, Kevin W., Francesco Abel, and John C. Harvey. *Birth, Suffering and Death: Catholic Perspectives at the Edges of Life.* Dordrecht: Kluwer Academic Publishers, 1992.

Wolf, Susan M. "Holding the Line on Euthanasia." *Hastings Center Report* Supplement (January /February 1989): 13–15.